Maxine Blake is of Ja
raised in Wolverham,
managed in educational establishments across the
country for 37 years before retiring in 2020. She holds a
Master of Education degree from the University of
Sheffield, focusing on post-16 education.

In her retirement, Maxine has become a professional
busy-body and continues to scrutinise student work both
nationally and internationally. She also sings with the
Sheffield Community Choir who appeared on stage with
Take That on their Greatest Hits tour. She dabbles in
piano playing and, even after a decade of practice, still
refuses to play for an audience of more than two.

Post-2020 madness she hopes to continue her journey
towards becoming a travel writer, as an excuse to see
more of the world... not that she needs one.

She lives in Sheffield with her husband and also her son,
who is fortunately or unfortunately still locked down
with them. Sometimes they join her on her comically
slow morning runs.

Don't Poo in the Pudding Bowl

Anecdotes from 13,414 days of teaching

By Maxine Blake

Don't Poo in the Pudding Bowl

ISBN 978-1-8383040-0-3

www.maxineblake.com

Cover design by Angelique 'Mostert' Boseman
@the.book.studio
Interior illustrations by Jo Titman
https://m.facebook.com/Jojitsu-106349327955595
Typesetting by David Fenton
Copy Editing by Rebecca Wojurska

A Teacher of Sport or a Teacher?

On receiving his feedback, a student responded, *"Maxine why are you correcting my grammar you're a sports teacher."*

I am a teacher.

MASTICATION

(Word of the day)

"...a technical word for the act of chewing"
https://www.dictionary.com

Sometimes I enjoyed confusing my students at the beginning of their lessons. The look on their faces as they confused it with the other MA word...

To Dave and Aaron

There would be no book without you. I'm forever grateful.

TABLE OF CONTENTS

PREFACE

My teaching career began in schools, two years had passed before I realised that I preferred to impart my knowledge to students aged sixteen and over.

I found myself facing classes of boys instead of girls; this demanded a whole mindset change They're all in that phase where their hormones are going crazy. With the boys though, the air is filled with testosterone, both in smell and attitude, and their heads are all over the place. They are cheeky, funny, irritating, sail close to the wind with their opinions, and they fart and dare you to mention it (I may yet delve into this). They continued to challenge me to physical contests, as if beating a middle-aged woman is a ticket to their manhood. So, after all of these years, I'm still not sure what they really see when they look at me.

My mid-term breaks and long summers have always been spent travelling the world making memories and having incredible explorations. They are no match to the adventures and shenanigans that often occur in the classroom though. My students bring a wealth of experiences with them from all over the globe, many under very difficult circumstances and they have taught me to keep in touch with my roots. They frequently involve me in passionate discussions on which nationality has the best Sunday dinners, who's the best cook in the class and more to the point, why am I not bringing in some home cooking for them to taste? Their varied experiences and the traditions from their home countries have been shared in the most unexpected of moments. My life has continued to be enriched by these small insights.

As most people do, to unwind at the end of the day I'd tell my family and friends of the latest things that happened at work. As these stories would spill from my mouth, often at a rate of knots, mouths would fall open, faces would look incredulous, some sceptics even dared to express that these events could never happen in an educational establishment. As I talked to family and colleagues, we would constantly say that the regular incidents that occurred at work, if written down, would make a great read and give insight into some of the activities that happened within our place of work. Needless to say, a few of the stories could never be for public consumption.

I was finally persuaded to write some of my stories by my son and husband, not because I could write a good story – I have no idea whether I can – but because of my personal relationships with the boys and the things that they continued to do and ask me, even thirty years later they still continue to amaze me. So, I decided to write as many of them as I could both sport and not sport-related – with a little help from my teacher friends and a few former students and pupils.

I hope that you enjoy the read.

DISCLAIMER

During the writing of this book, some names have been changed to minimise the student's embarrassment. On the other hand, some names have remained as the students have proudly accepted that their stories are worthy of being retold.

THE SKIRT INCIDENT

Schadenfreude

"..satisfaction or pleasure felt at someone else's misfortune..." https://www.dictionary.com

(Word of the day. This one's all about me)

It was a new academic year, and the class of level three (pre university) boys were still showing me their best side and were a delight to teach. I had decided to give them an in-class assessment (cruel I know, as I didn't have to) but just to be a little nicer, I allowed them access to textbooks for the latter half of the assessment.

I had just returned to work after a lengthy absence following my travels to Bolivia and Peru. I had picked up some bug or parasite, losing one and a half stone in the process over two weeks. I understand that many of you might say that losing weight is every woman's dream, but after a few weeks of still having to use the toilet and sink for simultaneous expulsions, you can understand that I desperately needed an end to this.

(I apologise for that image, which may stick for a while).

That morning at home, I tried on a number of different clothing options, thinking, should I wear my favourite shirt? No. too big. Hmm. I didn't need any more attention than is necessary when I had a class full of giddy hormonal seventeen-year-old boys. In the end, I chose a long knitted top that rested just above my knees (which helped to hide my out-of-control breast appendages) and teamed it with a skirt that settled nicely on my knees. You'll soon see where I'm going with this. Once in the classroom with my level three boys, and that assessment, I chose to place them in rows (old-school style) facing the front of the class, as opposed to their usual groupings of four to six in tables around the class. I then set them off on their assessment task.

After twenty minutes, one of my colleagues walked into the class, or I should say hobbled in as she too had been absent recently but with a bad back (not a great start for the sport staff). She walked towards the back of the class, where the tambour units were situated, to retrieve the textbooks for her next lesson. The lock can be a little tricky, and I didn't want her to aggravate her back any further, so I got up to help her.

As I stood up, I heard a rustling sound. The noise was unfamiliar so I couldn't place its origin and thought that it was in my mind.

As I began to walk down the centre of the class, I realised that the sound wasn't a figment of my imagination, as the noise was also travelling with me. The rustling continued to increase in both sound and pace, in time with my own strides. With each additional step, I my skirt was slowly making its way past my knees, almost Matrix style.

The noise, I soon realised, was my skirt lining succumbing to gravity and sliding down my legs. By the time my head had made the mental connection, my waistband had already passed my knees and was heading for the floor.

My head said, *You have two choices.* (I know what you're thinking: really, at this stage? You gave yourself options?) Yes, I had options, or so I thought...

Option 1

Step out of the skirt, put it over my shoulder and carry on walking as if nothing had happened (this was an obvious non starter).

Option 2

Slow down, pull the skirt up, hold onto it for dear life and make the best of a catastrophic moment.

My inner voice said, thank God (and I really was) you're a woman of colour or you would be a deep shade of red right now. Well, my whole body was on fire with embarrassment.

I chose option number two. Well, number one was a nonstarter. If at all possible, I needed to retain some semblance of dignity.

Remember I'd said that the boys were facing me? Slowly a few sniggers began to develop; my colleague Louise and I looked at each other. She noted my dilemma and looked mortified (we did that eye contact thing, my eyes said help, hers said s**t!). She quickly took control.

"What is your problem? You're supposed to be focussing on your assessment and impressing us with your knowledge. Just get on while me and Maxine sort out a little issue."

All eyes went down. It worked, or so I thought. Remember the students were new to the college and hadn't found their feet or voices yet.

Parts of my skirt had, by now, hit the floor. I carried on walking, stooped, and, with my left hand, grabbed my waistband that was now well below my knees. I lifted it up, closed the zip and continued slowly towards the tambour unit without a break in my stride pattern. I unlocked the unit, looked at Louise and exhaled then, after slowly returning to my seat, swivelled my chair towards the computer and stared at the screen as if it was normal practice.

Remember my clothing choices? Thank God for that long top.

The voice inside my head was gathering momentum (&*?>@<: *&^% &^%$££ – I'll let you provide your own interpretations here). There were really no words to express my emotions or situation.

Eventually, my inner voice said, *Note to self, get a safety pin later.*

I dismissed the class at the end of the session, knowing that facing them again a few hours later would be torturous.

The skirt incident happened at about 9.20 am, during the first session of the day. By a strange timetabling fluke, this was the only day of the week that I would see the class twice in a day, for the first and last lessons. By the last lesson, the news would have spread like wildfire. I thought, *How was I going to deal with this?* I mentally read the headlines: "Teacher exposes herself to a class of minors!" and "Students seek therapy after teacher exposure!"

How was I to face them again in the afternoon? I needed to put a plan together to get ahead of this the only way I knew how.

As I left the class, I began to tell key staff members and specifically the senior management team, as I needed to judge their reactions. As a member of management myself, I felt that I needed to get them on board. As I retold my story, mouths fell open, eyes widened, hands covered mouths and looks of sympathy and expressions of comfort were given. They all expressed how well I'd handled it, as they had no idea what they would have done in my position. So, I had the sympathy vote and hopefully no legal repercussions.

Plan A was complete.

Plan B was figuring out how to deal with the class. Well, I thought, there's no escaping this one. I'm going to have to take it on the chin. I've possibly lost all credibility as the no-nonsense, straight-talking teacher who always had situations under control. How am I going to get them to focus? I'm in a lose-lose situation. I'm going to be ridiculed every time I try to teach them.

14.20 pm came and with it my second lesson of the day with the boys. I prepared myself for what could be the worst day of my career, knowing I would have to withstand the barrage of quips and jokes that were going to be coming my way.

I walked up the corridor, participated in a little small talk with a few of them to try to gauge the atmosphere, and unlocked the door. They took their places and sat down, then I took the register and waited... waited for the atmosphere to change and for the comments to start. I braced myself for the impending attacks. I didn't even bother to recap the previous lesson.

Nothing.

I started the lesson (still nothing). No strange uncomfortable looks, no comments, no shuffling in their seats, just... nothing. The main section of the lesson... nothing. No recognition that anything untoward had happened previously. This is worse than a full-scale riot, I thought. I waited... still nothing. The lesson came and went with nothing more remarkable to add. I became increasingly more worried as this could only mean that they wanted me to suffer. Maybe it was already out in the public domain. If their parents found out the college would have to act. What should I do? My mind continued to work overtime.

I didn't wait around at work for any general chit-chat, but rushed home to tell my husband and son about my disastrous morning. I opened the door and went straight into the living room. There were no hello's, kisses or hugs. I went directly into my monologue about my wandering skirt, the boys lack of reaction and my colleague's support. There was no reaction; they hadn't heard a word that I'd said as they were busy doing stuff that boys and men do on their computers with their headphones on (I hadn't even noticed that when I entered). I continued to stand in front of them and carried on with what was by now developing into a rant. Then they realised that something out of the ordinary had happened. I reiterated loudly, *"IN MY LESSON TODAY WITH MY SEVENTEEN-YEAR-OLD BOYS, I STOOD UP TO HELP A COLLEAGUE AND MY SKIRT SLID DOWN PAST MY KNEES"*. They looked at me. There were no physical or verbal expressions of support, or even throw away comments of, "We feel your pain." Instead, they simultaneously logged onto Facebook, believing the pupils would have posted pictures or comments (this was definitely not what I was expecting).

"Surely it must be on here," my husband said. "They can't miss an opportunity like that." There was still no expression of concern or offers of support from either of them, just curiosity as to the amount of exposure (deliberate pun) that I would now be getting.

Nothing was posted. Well, that or they just could not find them.

Nothing was ever posted.

Over time, it dawned on me that the students were either so horrified by the episode that they had experienced group trauma and, to protect themselves, buried it deeply in their subconscious. Or perhaps they had heard of my Terminator title (one of my later stories) and wouldn't dare post their thoughts for fear of any repercussions. I'm still not sure which answer I'd prefer.

I continued to teach them for the rest of the year. There was nothing, not a hint or a flicker. I'm still lost for words. In fact, seven years later one of them started his teaching practice with us. This will be interesting, I thought.

Maybe after some adjustment time, I thought, he might just mention it in jest.

A year passed and there was still no mention of that day. I thought, Maybe I should reminisce with him and see if he brings it up. Then again, why ruin a young man's memory.

Whenever I taught the boys, I never wore those items of clothing again. My theory is that it was so horrific for them that should the said items of clothing be re-worn it would trigger deeply buried memories and drive us all into therapy.

IS THIS A COMPLIMENT?

"When you first came here, I thought you'd be really hard, but you're not."

1983: THE TRIALS BEGIN...

This was my first teaching job, and I was what was known as a newly qualified teacher (NQT). My new place of work was in such a state that I was being paid what I liked to call "danger money." This school needed additional assistance as it had one of the highest levels of deprivation within the country (hence the additional pay). There were constant streams of new initiatives, in addition to numerous experts throwing their ideas into the ring. Once you've read my story, you'll gain a better understanding for the reasons behind the need for the danger money. During the early days of my probationary period, I quickly realised that I needed to develop an armour of resilience or I wouldn't survive my first term, never mind my first year. My teaching degree had severely underprepared me for this; it was unlike any of the schools that I'd attended or taught at during my teaching practices. I clearly remembered my polytechnic lecturer's advice: if I took the job it would put me off teaching for life. In those early days, her words resonated frequently.

I obviously liked a challenge but, if I really thought about it, I desperately needed a job. The Head of Girls P.E. was off on long-term sick leave, so I was joined by a supply teacher as it was considered unsuitable for an NQT to run a department on their own. This was not a great start, regarding the essential support systems needed for a newly qualified teacher. The pupils suddenly had a young naïve black teacher and an aging white semi-retired teacher as their new P.E. staff. The school had a history of having no sporting activities outside of lessons (which I found equally reflected in the lack of structured activity in the lessons), there were no inner city or out-of-the-city sports events that it participated in, and the school's reputation for behaviour was at an all-time low.

The staff appeared to be lifers (i.e. been there a very long time). I wasn't sure whether that was good or bad, but I was soon to find out. The building was leaking, there were buckets everywhere, and some of the staff wore cut-off jeans and flip-flops to teach (standards!). Well, I was forewarned. The headteacher's didn't seem to last long, par for the course; they swept in, brought new initiatives to prove their worth and were gone before the inevitable disasters unfolded.

At the time there was no headteacher present, so an interim head was placed in position while yet another suitable candidate was found. The interim head came from the recently disbanded Sheffield Local Education Authority and was, by title, one of the two PE subject advisers who had responsibilities across the city. This type of situation was probably all too familiar in deprived schools across England. All I knew was that it was going to be an interesting and exciting journey, not the one that I expected. A familiar story, I'm sure, for many teachers.

Let's just say that the pupils and their families were a little unusual. My first tutor group included a girl who came in the thinnest of summer dresses with torn sleeves, worn-out shoes and no coat in the winter term, but her family owned a horse. Another pupil was often "loaned out" to his aunt and uncle in order to help increase their social security benefits. The estate from which some of the pupils came from was known nationally for its high crime rates and regularly featured in the local news, occasionally progressing onto the national news. You would never park your car in that area, just in case your wheels were stolen, but at least I knew who to ask in order to get them returned.

DON'T POO: THE PHANTOM CRAPPER STORIES

We had what we teachers called the development of "The Phantom Crapper Period." Rumours began to spread... well, not rumours, facts were described in sufficient detail to leave little to the imagination during our morning staff meetings. The issue? The latest location of the Phantom Crapper's deposits. The interim head squeamishly explained that one or more of our pupils needed psychological support, as their recent behaviour had resulted in what he described as an obsessive interest in Piaget's anal phase of development. This produced a myriad of responses from the staff. The more delicate staff closed their ears while from the corner came the announcement, *"You mean he's shitting in public."*

Chuckles would dissipate from a corner of the room, while other staff would hang their heads in despair. The Phantom Crapper's identity remained unknown for some time. You never knew where or when they would next strike, or who, if any, were the intended victims. An unfortunate teacher would occasionally enter the staffroom and have to account for their hastily changed clothing, and for that familiar lingering smell. Then, in their anger, declare that it was not help that the perpetrator needed, but a few timely reminders of their impending comeuppance (or words to that effect).

It was in the Phantom Crapper Period that we had a newly appointed headteacher (let's call him Mark T). His first initiative was to try and instil an air of equality within the school by asking the staff to call him Mark. In the same week, during the school assembly, he then nonchalantly introduced the staff to the pupils by our first names. We stood transfixed around the edges of the hall. You can just imagine the reactions of the lifers.

His next initiative was to continue with the middle-school ethos for the lower-school pupils by reducing the number of staff who taught them. He asked us if we would be willing to teach additional subjects outside of our specialisms. I volunteered as part of this experiment and said that I could teach Home Economics and Needlework (only because I could cook and sew). More on that soon.

Mark T's short reign came and went and we were still stuck with both the Phantom Crapper and the middle-school type teaching. Reading between the lines... he wasn't very successful. Our interim head returned to us but, to be honest, we would have welcomed anyone after Mark.

***

Karen

A brief introduction to Karen

Karen was the type of girl that teachers lovingly described as full of character, she was small and quite slim but when she was in a room, everyone knew about it. She had an answer to everything whether she had the required subject knowledge or not and everyone had to pay attention when she opened her mouth, or you would certainly regret it.

She was popular, well the whole school knew about her, and most staff were on tenterhooks when in her presence.

On this particular day, I was teaching in the Home Economics room. I began my lesson and things were going well when Karen entered the room, late as usual. This time was different though; she mumbled an apology, then immediately began to search the cupboards quite frantically. This disrupted the calm atmosphere of the class, but this girl was also prone to flying off the handle, so I had to approach her with care. Her feathered haircut: short above the ears and long at the back looked more frazzled than normal. As I tentatively approached her to encourage her to her station, she stopped, let out a call not too dissimilar to Archimedes' Eureka cry, and carefully cupped her hands around a pudding bowl. She turned and, before I could react, I found myself with the bowl and its contents directly under my nose.

"Miss, Miss, look what I've found."

She looked up at me beaming with delight and waited expectantly, her hands remaining outstretched under my nose. I took a step back as my olfactory system quickly identified the odour, resulting in my nostrils flaring. The contents were clear to see. Curling up from the middle of the bowl, finishing near the top with a swirl, was what could only be described on any other day as a bowl of beautifully presented Angels Delight (minus the smell of course). But this certainly wasn't that. I can put it in no other terms than to say it was a full bowl of s--t. There was no protocol for this. Karen was clearly delighted with her find and looked at me as though she was due her reward. The lesson immediately disintegrated, and I now had to swiftly deal with the situation. Ok, I thought, Liz, the Head of Needlework, is next door. I'll go there.

I interrupted her lesson and took her to one side to show her the bowl and its contents.

There was a pause.

"Is it steaming?" she asked.

That was not the question that I expected and, more importantly, was not the one I needed. Unsatisfied with that response, I took the offending object and went in search of the overall head of Home Economics.

She took the bowl and looked at it as though wondering whether she had mistakenly put sugar in her tea.

"Mmm, well we can just wash it out and return it to the cupboard."

On every level possible, there were so many things wrong with that response.

1. The actual washing of the poo/s--t/excrement from the bowl.
2. Where would the washing be done? Not where you prep food, surely?
3. Who would do the washing?

4.   Placing the bowl back in the cupboard, knowing that some unsuspecting pupils were going to mix food in it. Then the poor innocent families swallowing segments of it.

All of the above thoughts swiftly raced through my head.

"I'm not doing that!" I blurted out.

I couldn't believe what I'd heard from this highly respected woman. How could this be, in any shape or form, a reasonable response? I knew the roof was leaking and there were buckets on every corridor, but surely this was unworthy of money-saving action. My mind just couldn't comprehend her reaction. I made a mental note to myself: *if ever invited to her house, either refuse politely or don't touch any food. You never know what could have occupied the containers prior to the food being served in it.*

She really expected me to blindly follow her instructions, but I couldn't, so I had no choice but to take the bowl and its contents to the highest authority in the school: the headteacher's (or in this case the acting head) office for it to be dealt with. I explained the circumstances, offered the article up for inspection and examined his reaction (more out of curiosity than anything else). He placed said article on the table, turned and then left his office. I had no idea what he made of the situation, or what he did with the evidence.

Needless to say, the Phantom Crapper swiftly became a hero around school; pupils were wondering and laying bets on where they would strike next. In our staff meeting, our interim head once again reiterated the possibilities that our protagonist must be psychologically disturbed and would be in need of extended therapy once caught. He again urged staff to keep a look out. As if we weren't wary of every step that we took or were not trying to identify any changes in pupil behaviour. The lifers, with their names invisibly embroidered on their chairs, yet again took an alternative view.

"Bring back the cane."

"Those were the good old days."

Not too long after this, we had an unexpected breakthrough.

The head had an announcement to make. The Phantom Crapper had been caught by the caretaker. An unexpected hush rushed around the staffroom.

The head caretaker had literally landed himself in the s-- t.

My ears perked up. Apparently, the caretaker was on the school stage up in the eves, repairing the stage lights. Unbeknown to him, the Phantom Crapper had placed a freshly deposited pile in a dinner plate next to the bottom of the ladders. As the caretaker descended, he placed his foot straight into it (I know what you're thinking, *where the hell did he get the plate from?*). Apart from the continued disgust and lack of opportunity to capture the perpetrator, my mind had actually turned to the dinner plate, hoping that it wasn't from the Home Economics department, that the head of department would not find out and that it would not be returned to its rightful home. Another reason not to have lunch with the team in the base room.

But the Phantom Crapper had finally been caught, and not soon enough. I was fed up of walking with my head down to avoid what might be lurking around every corner. The perpetrator was actually caught by the caretaker mid his second deposit, so to speak, his trousers down to his ankles, full moon in view, on another section of the stage. Surely there can be no better site?

The Phantom Crapper was carted off to the acting heads office on his tiptoes, as his left ear was held so high between the fingers of the caretaker's hand, that his feet barely touched the floor. What took place next can only be described as the most bizarre meeting ever. The interim head was known for his softly softly approach, which was interesting enough during his first innings. I'm not sure how the powers-that-be thought that a second innings would improve matters but it was Hobson's choice unfortunately. He continued with his soft approach and asked his secretary to make a pot of tea for two while he and the perpetrator discussed the recent events. Apparently, he asked for the best china too. You can only imagine how the other pupils were thinking of what they needed to do to have tea in the head's office from that moment on.

RASHAWN AND ELIJAH: WHAT IS THAT ABOUT?

Rashawn and Elijah

A brief introduction to Rashawn and Elijah

As brothers from another mother they were always in each other's pockets. They had the gift of the gab, great eye contact, especially with the women, and dressed to impress. They always had a story to tell.

"Late to the lesson again, boys."

"Sorry Maxine, we had some tings to settle first that couldn't wait. You know what we mean." They both dipped their heads and winked at me. Unwilling to disrupt the class further, I let them settle and continued teaching the class.

Five minutes later, there's a knock at the door.

I opened the door. Two girls were standing sheepishly outside, trying to peep into the class. "Can we give these back to Rashawn and Elijah, please?" They held up the boy's jackets. I quickly retrieved them and handed them to the boys. My face tells them that an explanation is required later.

"You see, Maxine, it was their turn to carry our jackets around at lunchtime. They were just returning them now that their time was up."

Words were to be had later. I could bide my time.

JOEL: -PANTS, PROPOSALS AND OTHER STORIES

Joel

A brief introduction to Joel.

He walked with a swagger and a small gait, probably because his jeans were always fastened under his bottom. It gave him "a nice hitch", as he would say, meaning it accentuated his rear end. He had a softly spoken voice and eyelashes that curled all the way up to his eyebrows. There was that ever-present glint in his eye, whatever the situation. He was consistently late to class and always had an excuse, but when he arrived on time, the whole class knew about it. He collected trainers and once confessed to owning at least thirty pairs; my eyes watered when he revealed the price. I was never sure whether he should hook me up with a pair or report him as he was permanently broke. He also ordered a man bag from the "U S of A," as he liked to say from a notable designer. The shipping price alone would pay for most of my wardrobe. He wore his African heritage with pride and knew that this and his inventive patter would intrigue the girls.

Unnecessary Attention

While dropping his trousers, Joel said, "Maxine, do you mind if I get changed in the class? I was in a rush."

"I'd rather you didn't, Joel. It's inappropriate. While we're here, next time would you mind wearing trousers that are a little more loose." (I was trying to avoid dipping my eyes to the offending area). "You're causing unnecessary attention around the college."

He swaggered. "Well, it's like this, gotta show off my weapons innit? Anyway, I'm double bagged so it's ok."

All of that going on.

"Joel, did you know you had a hole in your underwear?"

His hands immediately reached for his bottom, frantically searching for the hole while simultaneously trying to pull his trousers up.

"Thanks. I just didn't need to see all of that going on," I said while circling my hand in the general area of his bottom.

Nuff Pants.

"You're still wearing yesterday's underwear, Joel."

"It's aaight init. I've got nuff pants of the same colour."

He swaggered off. In his mind he's swaggering but, with his joggers firmly hitched under his bottom to ensure both maximum exposure and to create the illusion of enlarged glutes, he only succeeded in drastically changing his gait to the point where he was forced to double his pace. Not too dissimilar to the appearance of someone who's about to be caught short of the toilet.

That Proposal

The last day of term and my students had assessments to complete and viva's to get through, so there was no respite for them. They were exceedingly quiet. I heard a strange noise not too dissimilar to rolling and bumping sounds. I eventually turned round to see Joel using a de-fluffing roller on Sahal.

"Please, no hair combing, affectionate grooming, waxing, or spraying in my class."

"Sorry, Maxine," came the multiple replies.

"Only because you've been caught," I said. To be honest, the silence was beginning to get to me, and I actually thought that it was quite humorous.

Fifteen minutes went by with more silence of the type where you suspect that they're up to something. They're always up to something.

"Yeh Maxine," Joel said. "Do you remember when I asked you to marry me when I was on the level two course?"

The whole class looked at me. I looked at him.

"No!"

"Yeh, Sahal, do you remember?"

"Oh, yeh I do," Sahal chipped in.

"You shut me down. You shut me down."

"Joel, that's wrong on so many levels. It's bigamy for one," I said.

"I don't even know what that means right now."

So, I explain it to him and to the class and add, "Never mind the teacher student thing!"

"Well, I'll be leaving soon and I'm nineteen."

I was getting nowhere here, so I had to close the conversation.

Another fifteen minutes later, I was marking Joel's work and called him up for some feedback.

"I'm really impressed with the eloquence of your written work and how you've managed to weave the theory into the practical."

Long pause.

"I don't even know what you're saying to me right now."

So, I broke it down again for him.

A large beam spread across his face.

"I'm gassed right now."

With an exaggerated swagger and nod to everyone as he passed them, he went back to his chair.

I guess he's happy then.

Anonymous

It was my duty day. I was in the plaza, as usual, having a chat with staff and students. We had created a games room in one corner of the plaza area, and it was enclosed in glass.

As I was chatting with the sports boys, Joel piped up and said, "Here's an anonymous tip for ya, there's a student in the games room with a box of food, just saying. She has her hood up." (The sign on the door read: no food or drink is allowed in here.)

He swaggered away. I stood there and thought, he has no idea what the word anonymous means. Then again, he couldn't define bigamy either. I smiled to myself and strolled into the afore mentioned room.

THE COTTON WOOL SANDWICH

Transubstantiation

".... the changing of the elements of the bread and wine...in theology."

https://www.dictionary.com

(Word of the day, for no reason whatsoever)

I was still teaching Home Economics and Needlework with a modicum of success. The class at the time were happily settled, completing plain and cross stitching with large needles on patches of hessian squares. The aim was to assess the levels of their manual dexterity and to identify their attention to detail before attempting more complicated sewing on the sewing machines.

I heard a squeal, followed by shouts of *"Miss Bleighke"* (Sheffield pronunciation for Blake). Anthony proceeded to jab me with his needle to attract my attention (it could have been so much worse). Unaware of the direction of the squeal, I wandered around the class reprimanding and managing minor issues. Then I heard the squeal again.

What now? I thought

"Miss, Miss. Karen's swallowed a needle." (Karen, 'the Poo Bowl finder')

"Ok... What?!" The message had suddenly registered in my head.

What the hell has she been doing?

It could perforate an organ, she could die.

What was she thinking?

I could feel the levels of panic rising within me.

Wait a minute, is this a wind up?

My mind was racing assessing multiple scenario's.

As I approached her, I looked at her face and realised it was true.

I told Karen not to move and asked a pupil to get the head of department. I stayed with her to make sure that she made no sudden movements. She didn't know what to do with herself, she kept twitching, trying to stand up. I almost had to sit on her to keep her still (I can hear you thinking, you can't do that. Different times remember?). I asked her what she was doing when this happened; she explained that she was getting more thread and popped the needle between her teeth, when someone made her laugh. She then ended with, "It's not serious, is it?" Viv (the head of department) came in to explain that she'd sent a pupil off to the staffroom to call for an ambulance.

Karen beamed. "Never been in an ambulance before. Me mam'll kill me though, coz I'm always gettin' in trouble." We decided between us that it was safe enough to escort her to the office to wait for the incoming ambulance. The ambulance arrived, Karen was assessed and taken off to hospital, and I went back to the class in an attempt to rescue the remainder of the lesson.

The following day, Karen returned to my class. I asked her about her hospital visit (her presence in school obviously indicated that she was fine).

"It were oreight, the' gimme an x-ray, saw't' needle 'n' gimme a cottun wul sarnie t' eat."

"Oh." I was a bit confused.

"Tole me to wait 'til it came out naturally, should tek a day or two at most and I need to mek sure that I faand it."

She watched my face.

"Oh, ok."

Then it dawned on me. My face screwed up at the realisation that she was going to have to search through her solid deposits until the needle was found.

Two days later: "Miss, Miss. I've got the needle, do ya want it back?"

It took me a few minutes to interpret what this meant. I replied, "No, thank you. Keep it as a memento."

"A what?"

I just walked away.

DANIEL: BLOW, DON'T SUCK

A brief introduction to Daniel.

Daniel was blond, tall and a little clumsy for a sports student. He had large feet and always appeared to be tripping over them, making him a target for ridicule in practical sessions. He was wonderfully polite and constantly aimed to please. He was also on the autistic spectrum. This resulted in the staff always running to his defence when they were aware of any untoward behaviour among the students.

One of our aims is to protect those who cannot protect themselves. There are (rare) times though, try as we might, when we lose our self-control too because the situation is just too funny. This was one such occasion.

I had scheduled a practical physiology lesson with the level three (advanced level) students. The aim was to complete a number of submaximal and maximal fitness tests to assess their oxygen uptake, levels of fitness, and to teach them how to take data and interpret measurements. One of the tests included the use of the treadmill and the students were to test their maximal O2 uptake. I demonstrated the safety points on the stationary treadmill with the V02 max kit: use of the safety clip, the nose clip, one-and two-way valves to measure CO_2 output and O_2 uptake (remember this bit). The students were to read through their instruction manuals, work in pairs on the various apparatus in the lab and, when their tests were completed, they were to write up their findings. They then had to rotate onto the next tests. The tests started smoothly; I walked round each station checking that the students were on task and completing them correctly. Within a short space of time, I began to hear strange sounds, which were initially unrecognisable. I stood still and scanned the room in an effort to identify the location. I then heard the sound of muffled laughter; most of the students had stopped testing and measuring and were all facing the same way.

I took their cue, quickly walked in the direction they were all facing, and soon saw the focus of the student's laughter; it seemed that Daniel had taken much of my safety information literally. He was running on the treadmill, his face as red as a beetroot, and he was going nowhere fast. An additional scan of the situation brought further clarity. The safety clip was correctly attached, his nose clip in place, the mouthpiece had been inserted into the volume bag, also correctly attached; but the treadmill had not been turned on (I hadn't turned it on in my demonstration). He was actually attempting to sprint on the stationary treadmill. All of his efforts were in vain as he was trying to produce movement through manually turning the electric treadmill belt around while achieving zero distance (the opposite of the test objective). This was not the only issue; as I watched the machine readings for gaseous uptake, I failed to understand the gas differentiation readings and the volume bag content. The machine had a recording of zero gases whereas it should have registered some CO_2 content at least. This was really strange. I then cast my eyes on the volume bag, which should have been contained a mixture of expelled gases and moisture from his lungs and, furthermore, should have been quite full. Not only was the bag flat, but it was almost inverted to the point of being sucked in on itself and was a fraction of its original size. I still couldn't figure out why this was happening.

I needed to re-examine Daniel's overall breathing techniques and, on closer inspection, I noticed that it was all wrong. He was actually sucking the air out of the bag, not blowing into it. My eyes rescanned the whole situation yet again, the valves were all connected in the right order, but the additional effort needed to manually turn the treadmill's conveyer belt resulted in a higher

CO2 build-up than I would have normally expected. Add that to the fact that he was breathing in the bag's contents. He was therefore breathing in more CO2 than expelling it. This was exactly the opposite of what should have been happening. He must have been desperate as he had been continuously gasping for air.

I could feel the build-up of laughter and pity simultaneously bubbling up internally as I watched the mayhem continue to unfold in front of my eyes, but I needed to retain some semblance of self-control. I would dissect the situation further some other time.

I asked myself: Which bit of any of the instructions did he not understand? What had his partner been doing?

I had to intervene as he looked as though he was about to combust. I walked up and tapped him on the shoulder to indicate that he needed to stop and take his mouthpiece and nose clip off. His legs immediately buckled under him as he spat the mouthpiece out, removed the nose clip and gasped for air.

With order restored once more, the students returned to their tasks. I gave myself a few minutes to regain self-control and, when Daniel had recovered sufficiently, I repeated the protocols to ensure that he fully understood them, including the importance of turning the treadmill on.

IT'S ALL ABOUT HYGIENE

Ted

A brief introduction to Ted

Girth wise, Ted was a little on the large size and quite a quiet student. He contributed little in class so it was difficult to get to know him quickly. He was studying and living away from home for the first time and on the surface, he seemed to be adjusting well.

My line manager had a situation and she wanted me to deal with it. I had recently taken up the position of manager of a new Sport HND (Higher National Diploma) course in a land-based college and was enjoying the challenges that came with the post. Her request was of course rhetorical, so I therefore had to comply. This was no ordinary request though. Over time, I had noticed that she developed a nervous giggle with limited eye contact when she approached me with a sensitive situation. This, I deduced, was one of those. All she said was that I needed to talk to one of my HND students about an unexpected event that had occurred earlier in the week during a fire drill. To gain further background information, I also needed to talk to one of the duty officers. That was it, there was no more information to be had, the duty officer was also a member of the teaching staff.

Of course, curiosity got the better of me and I couldn't wait to see what the issue was. I set off to find Jo, the afore mentioned duty manager/teacher, and asked her about the fire drill and if there was anything I needed to know.

Her facial expression immediately changed.

"Oh my God... You know how we have to complete a drill at the beginning of each semester? Well, the wardens decided to conduct one in the middle of the night to see how effective our systems were. All of the students came out, and we completed a register, then realised that one was still missing. We thought that maybe he'd been drinking so didn't hear the alarm, so one of the male wardens went to check on him. He knocked on the door but there was no answer, so he used his key to enter the room. As he opened the door, this awful smell hit his nose and he was nearly sick. He thought something had died in the room and had been left there festering for weeks, and that maybe the student was shacking up elsewhere. He then turned the lights on and discovered, to his horror, the student fast asleep in the room. He held his breath and woke him up to join the others outside."

I then realised what my job was. My stomach knotted as I wondered how to explain this to the student and realised why my line manager had sheepishly approached me.

The following day I walked into the room to teach the class. The students filed in, happily chatting away. The first thing they did was to open the windows, then they took their seats. We continued the lesson as normal, but my nose was now seeking out the foul smell that I knew was coming my way. Despite the chill in the air, no one complained, not even Ted (let's call him that) who sat near the front. The remaining students (his friends) were a good three to four rows back, all clustered together; surely he would realise that something was amiss? The room slowly began to fill with an odour that I couldn't fully place; the open windows only served to delay and filter the unbearable stench.

The lesson ended, and I asked Ted to stay behind. As I approached him, the smell intensified and I fought to keep my nostrils under control. I have a very good nose for smells and can usually identify the origins of many odours, for example the difference between fresh sweat from physical activity, new sweat on top of old sweat and sweat from anxiety or fear. This, however, was something else. I could not begin to decipher its origins. Not only was it very old, it had a mustiness/fustiness that went way way back, not unlike an unwashed body (meaning a number of untouched weeks) on top of unwashed clothes, mixed with the essence of male hormones that are still trying to find their base levels. This mix was almost unbearable, and I now understood why the wardens thought that something had died in his room. I knew that this discussion had to be quick and that it was going to be very tricky. I needed to get Ted to think about his hygiene problem without offending him and thought, How do I approach this?

I began with a ruse; I asked him how he was settling in, whether this was his first time away from home, and whether there were any issues that I could assist with. He couldn't think of anything relevant that required a discussion. I then thought, I just need to say it. So, I asked him about the fire drill and the strange smell that was discovered in his room. He replied that he hadn't noticed anything different. This still isn't working, I thought. Try a different tack then. So, I began to describe one of my personal experiences and went with: A friend had cooked a gorgeous dish for me (cauliflower sabji) containing fenugreek. I remember being woken up in the middle of the night by this horrible smell and looking at my husband as the source. I was mortified when I eventually realised that the offending odour was disseminating from me and not him. I felt that I was smelling so badly that my nightwear was immediately destined for the washing machine, bypassing the usual wash basket. That day, I also had to eat humble pie and apologise to my volleyball team for being the owner of such an awful smell, and that was before training had even begun! I was later to discover that the combination of my hormones with fenugreek was increasingly malodorous during the ensuing week. As much as I loved the meal, should I ever eat it again, I was self-quarantining.

If you've lost my train of thought here, the idea was to make Ted think that as he was away from home and possibly experimenting with new foods, then these could have caused some type of adverse reaction within his body. This might then be coming out in his pores and/or, possibly, he could also be washing his clothes at the wrong temperature (I'm being very polite here). This therefore could have had an accumulated negative impact. His face looked slightly puzzled as he tried to think of what it could be, but he remained nonplussed. I told him not to worry if nothing immediate came to mind, but while he couldn't recall what the actual issue was, in the meantime he should try to launder his clothes a little more frequently at the right temperature as this might help. I walked away hoping that not only had I managed to get some semblance of my message across with minimum embarrassment, but also hoping he had not noticed my desperate attempts at trying to disguise my revulsion at being in such close proximity with him for such an inordinate length of time.

I reported my meeting to my line manager and she appeared to be satisfied with the proceedings. It took a little time, but eventually windows were closed, and the students gathered together in one area with no comments ever to be heard from either side.

Samyia

A brief introduction.

She needs less drama in her life.

"Is there a manager here? I'd like to speak to a manager, please."

I looked around and thought, Yep, that'd be me then.

I stood up, both to talk to and to prevent the girl before me from taking over the office.

I ushered her out into the hallway where I was met with her backing crew, leaning against the wall and looking on expectantly.

Mmm, so her crew are waiting to see what I was going to do. She needed an audience.

"I'd like to make a complaint about a teacher," she spouted.

"Ok," I said, "but this has to be discussed in private."

She paused, gave me the look, as only a woman of African descent can. Another pause, then she ushered her friends away. They reluctantly shuffled on.

I waited until they were out of earshot.

"What is it that you'd like to complain about?"

"It's Cheryl," she said.

My ears pricked up. This could be bad.

"So, tell me what your problem is. I'm listening." What you as a reader need to know is that each official complaint is processed and investigated, then sent up the chain of command and further actions taken should it be deemed necessary. This was the first leg.

"She said I had a hygiene problem."

She was looking more bemused than angry or humiliated. So, I quizzed her.

"Do you know what this means?"

She squirmed, "Not really, but I didn't feel right as she was telling me."

I mentally took a step back as my nose began to twitch and flair, subconsciously searching for any whiff of odour.

This was more serious than I originally thought and was going to take some time, so I formally introduced myself and asked her name. "Samyia," she told me.

With that out of the way I began to question her on the event.

"Where did this take place?"

"In the class," she *said.*

"Who else was there?"

"No one. She asked everyone to leave at the end of the lesson."

Ok. Good, I thought, she got that right.

"What happened next?"

"She sat me down and said that she wanted to talk to me about something delicate."

So, here's how the story goes to the best of my knowledge.

Samyia is a Health and Social Care student. Some of her qualification involves placements in different settings. Cheryl had been to one of her placements to visit the student and talk to her supervisor (a fellow teacher). On discussing the progress of the student, the issue of the student's hygiene had reared its head and some of the small children didn't want to work closely with her.

Samyia continued and told me Cheryl had said to her: "Now that your placement has finished, there are a few things that we need to talk about, coming out of my discussions with your supervisor. Some of the children had complained that they didn't like to work closely with you." (She was known to be a little blunt). "Your supervisor thought that it was best for this discussion to take place with someone that Samyia knew at college."

Chery continued, "It's really important when you're out on your placement to present yourself well because you're not just showing the placement what type of person you are but, just as importantly, you are representing the college and letting them know how well we prepare our students. In this case we need to rectify the situation. Do you understand what I'm trying to say?"

"Yes," Samiya stated.

We didn't talk about it after that.

I could only imagine that she left the classroom confused and angry, as she had no idea what she was supposed to have done but that she had felt quite uncomfortable. Hence her arrival with her support group to my door.

I realised then that it was my job to explain further what the hygiene problem actually was. Her crew were still present, out of ear shot, but they now needed to go as this was about to get a little sensitive. I needed to think about how to explain this to her without causing anymore distress. I wasn't physically close to her and she was still wearing her coat so there were no immediate tell-tale smells.

I thought it was best to continue with the placement analogy in order to provide the additional context to my explanation. I lowered my voice and asked her about her placement, what she liked about it, what the children were like and how close they liked to get her. She explained how they liked to get really close, how they were sometimes trying to climb on her lap and were constantly surrounding her. I then took the opportunity to explain how, "when you are working really closely with other people in that way, it's really important that our bodies and clothes are really fresh because we are setting a good example for the children. We know that when children are that small, sometimes they can make comments really loudly without realising they can often embarrass others."

I then encouraged her to "think of a situation where a child has said something unkind to another one and you have had to have a word with both of them. You might have to comfort one child because they were upset and then have to talk to the other to explain what they'd done and how painful that was. Well, your teacher was trying to prevent that from happening to you."

I didn't explain it well enough and she still failed to understand. I thought, grab the bull by the horns and tell it to her straight.

I said, "Imagine if it was story time and you wanted the children to sit close to you so that you could see the expression on their faces and help them to take part in the story. How would you feel if one of the children did not want to move any closer and started to get upset? When you ask her what's wrong, she replies 'I don't want to, you smell funny.'"

Her eyes widened and her mouth fell open. The penny had dropped.

Long pause.

"Will you tell me if I smell?" she blurted out.

"Of course."

I ushered her into the first available room.

I closed the door, making sure that no one could see us through the glass panelling.

We faced each other and, as she began to lift her arms up to take her jacket off, something strange happened.

This may now seem like a commercial break, but this is exactly the imagery being played out in my head. People of a certain age will be able to relate to this. Remember the Bisto kids, who were always out playing, only to be drawn home by the amazing trail of Bisto gravy that wafted in front of their noses and led them home? Well, it was something like that, only not pleasant at all.

As Samyia lifted her arms, that smell hit my nose; my nostrils flared, my eyes watered, I felt myself physically retract and quickly placed her arms at her side, leaving her with her jacket hitched at her elbows, mid arm.

s--t, I thought. First, that reaction wasn't good and, second, that odour is so bad that I can't even relate to the different smell intensities that were assaulting my senses.

I looked at her and quickly apologised for stopping her mid flow. I immediately stated that we didn't need to pursue this any further (as if I was a GP giving a medical opinion). She continued to stare at me. I continued to look at her.

"Well," I said, "your jacket isn't leather, is it? And your blouse looks like it's made from a mix of synthetic fibres."

I'm trying to buy myself more time here.

"When you have these synthetic mixes that meet the skin, they don't allow the skin to breathe. So, what could be happening, is that as you sweat and it dries and the cycle repeats, the fact that your clothing can't breathe means that additional bacteria will build up, causing an odour. In addition, where there are young children the rooms can be quite warm, causing you to sweat more often than usual." (I was really hoping that she was buying this answer).

"Oh, I see." Pause. "And I've had to run up the stairs today, making me very hot and sweaty," she added.

"Also, if you wear the same clothing the next day without it being washed and you've already got a bacterial build up, the smell then develops much more quickly than usual."

"Thank you so much for explaining this to me, Miss. Do you have any antiperspirant that I could use?"

I almost recoiled again.

"No, the worst thing that you could do now is add any underarm spray because the combination of smells would be even worse. The best thing to do is to nip to the toilets, get some soap, give your armpits a good wash and dry, and that will improve the situation greatly."

"Thank you so much for telling me again, Miss. I'm really grateful."

Off she went with a smile and a lighter step, down the corridor. I allowed myself a small grin as I felt that I had saved what could have been a catastrophic situation. Not only had I handled the incident well (mostly), more importantly, although she wasn't told the actual truth, Samyia could now go away and think a little more about her personal hygiene. At least she would come to the conclusion that she wasn't really humiliated by Cheryl and might even begin to address her personal situation.

I explained the incident to my line manager and regaled of how I single-handedly quelled a minor mutiny.

A few uneventful days passed with nothing to report, and I had almost forgotten about the incident (except that I kept catching myself holding my breath as I walked around college, particularly on the stairs, although I have no idea why that place).

Later, I had finished teaching a lesson and began to lock my door when I heard a familiar voice. Opposite my class was the staffroom. There Samyia was, asking, "Can I speak to Cheryl please?" I froze and waited to see what would unfold. It might have been nothing, but I wasn't betting on that outcome.

Cheryl came to the door and Samyia said, "Hi Cheryl. Do you remember when you had a word with me the other day after placement?"

"Yes," Cheryl confirmed.

"Well, I thought about it, and I still didn't really understand what you were trying to say. Would you mind repeating it again for me, please?"

I should have been pleased with this progress; she had approached Cheryl politely, asked her to clarify the previous situation, as she was still confused, so she could she go through it with her again. But this picture didn't look right... something was bugging me. So, I maintained my watch and listened in on the conversation. The eye contact between both parties looked positive, there were nods, exclamations, and a few repeats when Samyia still didn't understand. Then, I spotted it; my eyes were being drawn down towards her left hand in her pocket, which seemed to be fiddling a lot. It might have been nothing, but my suspicions were now stirring even more. The conversation finished and Cheryl retreated to the staffroom.

"Yes!" Samyia said. "Got you now."

She then took her phone out of her pocket.

That was it, I realised what was bugging me. The sneaky conniving little minx had been recording the conversation all that time.

I wondered what she was intending to do with it.

She walked… no, skipped, bounced, danced and fist pumped her way down the corridor where her friends were eagerly waiting. "Well?" one of them asked.

"Got it," she said.

What the hell! My head was spinning; this was pre-meditated revenge. I tried to remember what this situation was called again (I always struggled with the concept). Then it came to me: entrapment. I'd seen the film with Catherine Zeta Jones. I tried to remember if it ended well.

All I knew was that my triumph was short-lived, and I was not letting Samyia get the best of me. The time for being nice and supportive was over. I'm sure that there are textbooks methods for handling this kind of situation, but nothing was coming to mind. While Samyia and her crew were busy celebrating, I casually walked up to her and tapped her on the shoulder.

She quickly turned around.

"Hi Samyia, you seem to be in a much better place than when I last saw you," I said.

"Yes. thanks."

"It's a little bit noisy here, can I talk to you for a few minutes, please?"

"Sure." She excused herself from her friends and I quickly found a room.

I turned to face her; she returned my gaze and realised that all was not well.

"What do you intend to do with the recorded conversation between you and Cheryl?"

"Wha..."

hand up and stopped her mid flow.

erything. From the time you knocked on the door, to the celebrations with your friends."

"Well, she can't be allowed to get away with humiliating me like that. I'm getting my own back."

"So exactly where were you thinking of putting that information then? On social media? Well?"

I was becoming impatient.

She tried to formulate some kind of answer, but I wasn't giving her the opportunity to do so despite asking the question.

I took a breath, "Let me tell you how this can play out. At the moment, only you, Cheryl and myself know that this was about your personal hygiene issues."

(I really wanted to tell her how it was and get back to the basics of how soap and water are free and you should use it, as my mom would say, but I was still trying to maintain a modicum of professional decorum and finding it hard to do so).

What I said instead was, "If you place this on Facebook or any other social media forum, it won't just be the three of us who know about your issue, but your friends, your friends friends, and on and on it will go. Is that what you wanted?"

The penny dropped, her eyes widened, and her mouth fell open again.

"And another thing," (I was on a roll now), "what you just did was called entrapment. It is against the law and, not only is this now a college disciplinary matter, it can be a police matter. You can be privately prosecuted and, as a college, it will be out of our hands."

She had to take a seat. I gave her a few minutes to collect her thoughts.

"I only wanted to give her a taste of her own medicine, because I didn't like what she said to me."

I again explained how these kinds of situations were difficult to deal with and that it was Cheryl's duty to try to sort this out as quickly as possible while trying not to cause offence. I then explained that because of this new development, the situation would have to be taken further with my line manager and that we would discuss which level of the college's disciplinary process she would be taken through. I let her know that things would be made easier for her if she deleted the information and discontinued any of her planned actions. She was again very grateful for this option and continued to thank me for being so considerate up to the point when she left the room.

I stood and let out a huge sigh of relief, then went to see my manager.

I began to explain the incident, how having thought it had been solved, instead I'd stirred up a hornet's nest. Apparently, that wasn't the only thing that Samyia had been doing though. While I was dealing with that situation, Gail was dealing with another one. She was called into a health class where a teacher had discovered a petition going round the classes demanding that Cheryl should be sacked.

Needless to say, my promise that things would be easier for her if she ceased her revenge antics had now flown straight out of the window. With the multiple issues now going on, this had to escalate straight to the final stage of disciplinary.

So much for my effective management skills.

SKIRTING AROUND

Sarah

A brief introduction to Sarah

She was a little bit ditsy, as a thirteen year old, she was physically mature, her brain though had not yet caught up with her body. Unlike most of her peers who tried to dodge P.E. lessons at every given opportunity, Sarah welcomed them with open arms. She was always eager to please and volunteered often to help to demonstrate in practical sessions. Alas, these were not her forte

P.E. staff always have additional kit for when the time came (most days), that pupils "forgot" their own. This increased dramatically at the onset of puberty for most girls. At times there seemed to be more girls sitting out than participating in a lesson. So, I always tried to be accommodating and help them out whenever possible. There was one girl, Sarah, who was a little challenging at times as it always took slightly longer to explain the rudimentary points to her. Often girls would wait until the very last minute to explain their lack of kit, in the hope of being given other tasks to do instead of having to participate in the lesson. Not Sarah.

One day, she came bounding up at the beginning of the lesson to explain that she had forgotten her skirt but, during the break, had managed to borrow her sister's. Normally, this event wouldn't be noteworthy except for one key point: Sarah and sister had contrasting body types. Her sister, despite being a year older, had not yet begun any physical signs of maturation and was still the archetypal pencil-thin girl. Sarah, however, was an early developer, quite curvy and very busty.

With this in mind, I asked her if she was sure that she wanted to use her sister's skirt as we had others that she could use, but she put me at ease by stating that she had used her sister's skirt before and that there was no problem. The skirts were a simple A-line design with an elasticated waist that could be slipped on easily.

The lesson started and ended fine with no major issues. The girls then returned to the changing rooms to prepare for their next lessons. I was in my office handing out the jewellery when a fellow pupil announced that Sarah needed some help. I was not sure what that meant, so went to find out what the problem was.

Sarah was in the middle of the changing room with her sister's skirt quite firmly stuck onto her chest (with no wriggle room). She had already removed her P.E. top and was wearing little else. I examined the situation and thought surely if she had put it on easily, she should have been able to take it off easily too. So, I tried pulling it over her head and almost lifted her off her feet, then tried pulling in the opposite direction, but just succeeded in making her more uncomfortable as her skirt was squashed even more tightly onto her chest. She began to wail and scream, stating how her mom and sister were going to kill her as she had borrowed the skirt without asking. I asked her how she got into the skirt. She replied that she stepped into it but then decided to take it off over her head, and that's when it got stuck.

I let the rest of the girls go, as they would have been late for their next lesson but kept an additional girl behind. I stood in the middle of the room with Sarah. I needed to be careful as the skirt was well and truly secured onto her and I could be accused of all sorts. I was also acutely aware that she also still standing there in her underwear including her regulation navy-blue knickers.

I had exhausted all possibilities and felt that I was left with no choice but to call the head of the girl's upper school and ask for assistance. I didn't want to make any more decisions that could possibly incriminate myself. The head duly arrived and we dismissed the other pupil. Sarah's distress and crying had now visibly increased once she had seen who had walked through the door. The head paraded around Sarah as though she was a dummy in a shop window. I explained the situation and the actions taken so far, confirming that I had now exhausted all possibilities.

We eventually decided that we had no choice but to cut it off. I had that idea in mind but didn't want to pursue it because of the parent's possible reactions. I found a pair of scissors, gently cutting along the seams but being careful not to cut anything else on my way up. Sarah was released unharmed. A note was to be written by the secretary to the parents explaining the matter with the opportunity for further discussion should they need it.

Sarah never forgot her skirt again and I never heard of any comeback from her mom or sister.

WHO DO I REPORT THIS TO?

The athletics track was at the back of the college buildings. Jayne was teaching and had noticed a student running around the track. His look portrayed desperation more than it did exhaustion. She needed a word with him.

"Stop."

Then, a few minutes later, again, "Stop."

Eventually he stopped.

"Why didn't you stop?"

"He wouldn't let me."

"Who?"

Before he could answer, she noticed that his levels of distress had severely increased.

Jane thought he wasn't bright or quick enough to lie, so she quickly organised cover for the remainder of the lesson. She was escorted to the porter cabin by the student and he nervously pointed to the bottom of the cabin. Jane followed the direction of his hand and noticed a movement.

"Come out," she shouted.

She noted a pair of eyes peer at her from beneath the cabin, and saw he had some kind of shooting implement in his hands. Jane recognised the student and coaxed him out. He looked as though he had been on an assault course and admitted he was willingly shooting at the aforementioned student while he was running. Unphased by both his confession and the implement, she relieved him of the weapon and escorted him to the head of Student Services. Together, they decided that this needed urgent attention and escorted the student to his house. On discussion with his parents, the father said, "Yes, the rifle's ours." Then, turning to their son he added, "Why did you do that? Don't do it again."

And that was it.

Not exactly the response expected or required. They explained to the parents that the incident would need to be followed up by the college and would have to be reported to the police. The parents appeared to be nonplussed by this. Having left his house, they retreated to pay a visit to the student's house, who had been the unfortunate target, to explain his mental and physical state to his family. On being invited into the home, they were presented with a man and two women. They were confused, so Jayne asked who was responsible for the student. The man replied, "You can talk to any of us, we're all sharing the same bed."

It transpired that the two women were sisters. They all lived in a one bedroomed flat with the student using the settee as a bed. Again, not the response or reception that they had expected. The issue then was not only who do they report this to, but what do I report? To whom do I report it? In what order and when?

DAVE'S CHUNTERING TIRADE

It was the end of the school year and some of the pupils were being treated with a trip to Alton Towers. It was a particularly hot day resulting in a scorching, sweaty and crowded environment.

Dave, my husband, was present to make up the correct ratio of responsible adults to pupils, and he liked the idea of a trip where he had little responsibility. Oblivion was the newly opened ride, and we were keen to see what all the hype was about. The queues were long everywhere. We were frustrated not only with the heat and lack of shade but, having already queued for over an hour with at least another to go, people started queue jumping. Dave's increased levels of chuntering in particular was noted by my pupils nearby. They'd previously witnessed him walk towards an unknown group of pupils whose attempt to sneak in front of us was swiftly quashed as he marched up to them and ordered them to the back. I'd never seen them so quiet. Four of their friends sauntered up to jump the queue under the usual rouse of a chat. Dave was about to unleash another tirade when I heard one of the girls say, "I don't mind if you come in front of us, but I think he will." They slowly turned and looked, only to be faced with my husband glaring back at them. Enough said. They reluctantly made their way to the back of the queue.

DUMB AND DUMBER

I found myself embroiled in yet another interesting classroom scenario with my colleague Louise, with whom I shared the skirt exposure scene. We happened to be teaching in neighbouring classrooms and, as we approached our rooms, we had our usual exchanges of banter about who we were teaching, the characters among them and the varying difficulties of our approaching lessons. We exchanged this for a few minutes and mentally prepared ourselves for our upcoming classes.

Halfway through my lesson, there was a sudden burst of noise (raised voices) from next door, and a simultaneous scraping of furniture. I continued to teach. I raised my voice to drown out what now appeared to my students to be of more interest to them than my lesson. I then heard my colleague's raised voice (so did my students), and then I heard her students. The sounds of teacher, students and furniture had gathered momentum to such an extent that I could no longer ignore it. I left my students and rushed out of the class just in time to see a student (let's call him Darren) bounding up the stairs. To say that he was not himself is to underplay the whole situation.

Before I continue this story, let me take you through a small potted history of my colleague's class. For some reason, this year she had a combination of the most volatile students. Anything could set them off, so everyone needed to tread lightly. The student in question needed medication to keep him calm, docile and focussed while at college. Today he had forgotten his meds. His peers recognised the signs well enough and so took the opportunity to see how far they could go with him.

Throughout the day he had been putting up with all manner of jibes and jokes, none of which he could really understand. All he knew was that he was becoming hot, bothered, irritated, and was ready to blow. It was now the afternoon session. He was sitting opposite one particular fellow student who was being very vocal, so Darren decided that he couldn't stand it any longer. There was no obvious build-up to warn the teacher, but he was dealing with this the only way he knew how: with violence.

He jumped across the table and began to pummel the student with everything he had. They were eventually separated by my colleague and some of the class. He then dashed up the stairs. Why? No one knows.

Security was called.

This is where I came in. Louise was obviously upset and shaken. I entered the room just as Darren was running up the stairs and thought the drama was over.

Still no security.

We were discussing our options while standing between the class and the corridor. I was checking that she was ok and had propped myself up in the doorway, facing the class with my back to the corridor.

Still no security. I thought, what has to happen for them to turn up?

What happened next was such a blur. I often find it difficult to explain, but what I know is this: having gathered momentum from the top of the stairs, Darren appeared. He was partly through the door, between my colleague and myself, and was ready to continue his attack on the offending student.

Before I had registered what was really happening, I had him in an arm lock, face down on the table next to me. I had no idea how it happened. I held him there, as I couldn't think of what else to do. The class were still inside and stunned into silence.

A minute or so later, having run up the stairs, two very red-faced out-of-puff security staff approached the room. I looked at them, they looked at me, then they perused the situation.

"Where were you?" I shouted.

The first one (Dumb) said, "I went to get backup."

Dumber, having strategically placed himself behind Dumb, stood there, sheepishly grinning at me, and had nothing to say.

I looked at him, then at my colleague, as I couldn't really comprehend the message that he was actually trying to relay to me.

"Backup? **YOU'RE MY BACKUP**."

The fact that I was still holding Darren in an arm lock wasn't lost on them.

The class was no longer silent. As soon as they were told they could go, the stories spread like wildfire on how I singlehandedly managed to physically stop a student by using martial arts/wrestling/cage fighting. In fact, "Maxine terminated him single handed," while Dumb and Dumber, as they were then labelled, looked on. By the end of the day the stories had spread around the building on how Maxine "The Terminator" had saved the day.

Of course, I discouraged the embellished stories about my cage fighting/martial arts arm lock (it sounded more like I'd assaulted Darren). My Terminator title and the embellished stories of that day, however, remained for some time though.

CARL AND THAT INCIDENT

Carl

A brief introduction to Carl.

Carl was equally popular with the boys and girls in the school. He demonstrated just the right amount of confidence that made everyone feel at ease around him. He was never afraid to ask advice and try out new things. He was not afraid to fail but put his hand to everything to experience what life had to offer. He often had a huge welcoming smile and when he did, most of his teeth were on display and putting everyone at ease.

This group of pupils made a positive mark on me in my early years of teaching. I bump into them from time to time and exchange fond memories of that happy period. I remember a lesson that I taught in the sports hall, with an unexpected outcome. The class was split in half with one group on the trampoline and the second on the floor working on various gymnastic skills. One of the students was a club level gymnast and she was going through some of her advanced moves. This week's theme was round off to back flip. The gymnastics and trampolining equipment were close together, so I could teach and keep my eyes on both groups. Carl was keen to improve his gymnastic skills, so together Dawn and I coached him through the individual skill sections of the moves; when we were satisfied, we would put them together. The floor area consisted of the usual gym mats covering the practical sections, with crash mats around the perimeter that were to be pushed in when he landed. All was going well as I watched and coached. The round off to black flip was not the most aesthetically pleasing of moves but I was impressed both with my teaching and Dawn's keen eye. Carl was able to link the skills together quite quickly. I had noticed that Carl's elder brother Philip and his friend, Charlie, had somehow snuck into the gym (there were no free lessons, so their teacher had also possibly failed to notice their disappearance). Although they were generally good pupils, their appearance didn't help the lessons ambience (young, impressionable girls and a younger brother willing to show off), so I needed to have a quiet word with them later as I couldn't leave my station. The end of the lesson was approaching, so we were winding the class up and calling a halt to the gymnastics. As I began to walk towards the trampoline, Carl decided that he wanted one last attempt (not too dissimilar to the last run of the day on the ski slopes, often disastrous due to underestimated fatigue levels).

As I turned, I watched his run-up develop and, as soon as I saw his first-hand placement, I knew something was amiss. All I could do was to watch as the full sequence unfolded.

Hand placement, handspring, back flip, crashmats pushed in... then he landed.

This was different; he was slightly off centre, one foot had hit the crashmat, the other had hit the gym mat... or so I thought. In fact, his foot hadn't hit the gym mat, his knee had. We all froze as he laid motionless on the floor. There was no sound. The helpers just stopped, the other pupils on the benches were silent. I watched the colour fade from their faces as they froze in shock. One of them was his brother, Philip.

I ran over to assess him. Carl was lying on his right side in the foetal position holding his left leg. In my haste, I called for two ambulances but no one moved, so I had to shout to Philip and Charlie to go to reception and phone for the ambulance. My thoughts were that if I could get his brother out of the way, then I could manage Carl's situation more effectively and control the possible hysteria that might develop with the other pupils.

That backfired as the adrenalin must have worn off in Carl's body and he began to roll around and scream. I initially thought he had broken his femur (the upper leg long bone), but I was wrong. I could see the end of his femur (I shouldn't be able to, s--t), then just below that I could also see the end of his shin bone (the tibia).

In between was a gaping hole. His skin had puckered up and sucked itself inside; it looked as though someone had used the nozzle of a vacuum cleaner from the back of his knee and sucked the air out. There was also something else amiss with this picture... where was his kneecap?

His skin had re-formed tightly around the end of his bones and been sucked into the newly created void in the middle. Seriously, where the hell was his kneecap? As I leant over him, I finally saw it. It had found itself a new home on the outside of his left leg, still under his skin, and was now clearly in four pieces. No wonder the kids were in shock. As the noise from Carl increased, so did his movement. I realised that if I didn't do something fast he could sever or trap a nerve, causing further possibly irreparable damage. The only way to immobilise him, or so I thought, was to lay across his body. Everyone else remained stuck in their seats, which was a much better picture than the one of everyone running around screaming. It felt as though I had been positioned like this forever as I tried to soothe Carl and keep him calm until the ambulance's arrival. When they eventually arrived, and two still did, they had to prise me off him. Come to think of it, I don't recall any other members of staff being present; they probably were but all I can recall is the total inactivity of the pupils.

The paramedics assessed the situation and gave Carl gas and air. One stayed at his head, another took hold of his left leg and slowly began to straighten it. I looked, first in horror as I didn't think that you were supposed to do that (basic first aid training), then in fascination as the four parts of his kneecap slowly tracked themselves back to their original position between his tib and femur, then popped back into the hole. He was eventually taken to hospital where he had a pot put on (plaster cast) and lived to gain a hero's welcome back at school.

CHARLIE (TO WHOM I'LL BE FOREVER GRATEFUL)

Charlie

A brief introduction to Charlie.

Charlie was dependable, he was the quiet unassuming pupil that everyone could trust. He never made it an issue when he saved the day, this appeared to be more often than not. he just took it in his stride. His friends and teachers relied on him for different reasons. His friends, to back them up; the staff to keep the peace. He was always there when you least expected it.

Anthony

A brief introduction to Anthony

He was mischievous, always in the middle of things and appeared to live on the edge. His smile and the way he looked at you would get him out of trouble. He exclaimed to be the King of everything without having much knowledge of it, his friends believed it and followed him everywhere

This story again centres around trampolining and expresses my gratitude to Charlie for his speedy reactions and for covering my inability to be everywhere at once.

This was one of the first few trampolining lessons, so only the basics were still being taught. The pupils had previously been taught how to spot. There's always someone who thinks that they know more than they actually do and can do more than they have been taught (it's usually one of the boys). This time it was Anthony. Back drops were the limit at this time, but he was desperate to complete a front summersault. This is a tougher move than a back summersault as its more difficult to spot. It also requires the teacher to be on the trampoline to ensure that the correct movements are performed. Although this minimises the issues on the trampoline, it also maximises the opportunity for any misbehaviour around the bed. This class was not yet ready for that. Anthony, without my permission, decided that the move was easy enough and he was ready to give it a go. It was perfectly timed as I was at the far end of the bed and he was facing away from me.

He attempted the front summersault, neither knowing how to spot or land correctly. He landed on the balls of his feet and shot forward. All I could do was watch – all any of us could do was to watch – as the spotters couldn't save him as he sailed over their heads. Charlie – reliable sturdy Charlie – took a few steps backwards, opened up his arms and caught him, then helped him to the floor. He wasn't one for words and he said nothing. I was too stunned to speak for some time as all I could do was visualise Anthony spread-eagled on the floor and me jobless, in front of the court for having no control over my pupils. Anthony landed, brushed himself down, swaggered, spread his arms out to take the applause... as he'd planned it all of course.

Anthony didn't learn from this and continued to take risks wherever possible. As staff we had to complete lunchtime duties, so I was allocated the youth club area. The pupils were normally huddled in corners chatting or playing table tennis. Anthony decided that he'd try the latest dance craze because, of course, he was an expert. I watched him place a mat on the floor, curious as to what he was up to now (he was always up to something). He began with a basic backspin. Ok, I thought, this is quite harmless. As the crowd developed, he thought he'd expand his repartee. Before I realised what was unfolding, he was on his head, moving his body into a twist position then into a head spin. He slipped and landed on his neck. The pupils gasped. Once again, I visualised my career in tatters. The ambulance was called. Anthony smiled and looked at me sheepishly as he was stretchered away into the awaiting vehicle.

There ended Anthony's reign as the self-proclaimed king of break-dancing.

I walked past Ice Sheffield a few years ago, only to see a picture of an ideal family advertising sessions at the rink. There was a face I recognised on the picture. There Anthony was, in the limelight again, this time representing the modern family. I just wondered what he told his partner and children about his schooldays.

Anthony (just spell my name right, with an h)

Fast forward to July 2018, about 34 years later. I stood in a very crowded room of the young and not-so-young, who had gathered together to remember a well-loved member of the community. I tapped a man on the shoulder and said, "Anthony." A huge smile immediately spreads across his face.

"My God, Maxine Blake... you haven't changed."

I thanked him.

We exchanged thoughts on the mixed feelings of the occasion and how it brings everyone together. We reminisced on school pupils, who he was still in contact with, how they were and so on.

Eventually, I explained to him that after all these years, I'm writing a book on my experiences as a teacher; only humorous ones I hastened to add. He steps back and gives me that look.

He paused.

"Am I in it?"

"Of course you are." I gave him a run down and he chuckled. I then explained how I didn't want to embarrass anyone should it eventually get published and that I'd changed the names.

"No, don't bother, just make sure that you spell my name right. Anthony with an h in it. People always get it wrong."

I chuckled and commented that he hadn't changed at all, even mentioning the poster with his kids outside Ice Sheffield.

He looked at me and paused again, then asked, "Was I a naughty kid at school?"

"More of a mischievous child," I carefully replied. "You were a little challenging and you liked to think that you could do anything. Remember your breakdancing?"

He just nodded and grinned, then showed me a picture of his fifteen-year-old daughter, I looked at him and said, "Wow, you need to be careful, she looks much older than her years."

"I'm celebrating my fiftieth birthday soon," he mentioned. I stopped and thought, how is that possible? How can an ex-pupil of mine be so old? What does that make me then?

I congratulated him on his pending celebrations and wished him well, hoping to see him soon.

I then walked further through the room and spotted another ex-pupil. We looked at each other, gave each other the biggest hug and burst into mutual praise. I told him how impressed I was with his musical career, that I'd seen him on stage and on the TV recently, and how it filled me with pride. He then really surprised and stunned me when he retorted how I was his mentor and he had always looked up to me.

I had no idea and felt an amazing sense of accomplishment when I realised I had some part to play in helping shape someone to become such a wonderful human being.

FARTING PIGEON'S

Sternocleidomastoids

"… a thick muscle on each side of the neck…"

https://www.dictionary.com

(Word of the day) This one always drives the students crazy

Sahal

A brief introduction to Sahal.

On our first meeting, Sahal proclaimed that he wanted to find a wife by the time he was eighteen and have many children. He was tall, stood proud, would never hesitate to talk about his Somalian background. He walked as if he owned the soil that he trod on. With his chest held high, when he smiled there was almost a 'Colgate' twinkle emanating from his teeth. He loved himself and his group loved him.

Abdi

A brief introduction

He was the opposite in stature to Sahal and had a quiet self confidence. He was our go to self taught techie when we frequently had trouble with the various technological systems in college. He was painfully polite with a quiet spoken voice.

During another anatomy lesson, a group of boys asked me to settle a dispute that was developing on their table. I was hoping that there might at least be some semblance of the conversation relating to the subject matter. As they continued to disrupt my teaching, I asked them to explain the issue to the class (I used this as a re-focussing tool to halt conversations that are often not for my delicate ears). This just encouraged them even more, so I looked at the table where Sahal, Joel and Abdi were sitting. Joel explained he had been trying to settle the dispute but that the other two were not having any of it. Realising that this would not go away and thinking that I could solve this quickly, I let them expand further. Abdi stated, "It's true, I've seen it happen". The class was still no wiser, then Sahal held court. He slowly looked around the class, gave his usual big grin, puffed up his chest, paused for effect, then began: "It's true Maxine. When a pigeon farts on another pigeon, it becomes pregnant."

He wasn't questioning me, this was rhetorical. I couldn't respond. I just didn't see that one coming. Abdi continued to back him up and I'm not even sure that Joel was fully convinced that this statement wasn't factual.

I fell against the window and gave no apology for the spontaneous laughter that came out of me. I actually said that if I wasn't supported by the window ledge I would have fallen over.

Just for clarification, I asked them to repeat their points. I then let my eyes roam around the class. There were no strange looks, alarmed sounds or ridicule; in fact, the only reply came from Demi who calmly told them not to be so ridiculous. All that I could say was that if they believed that, then I had much more work to do than I had originally thought. They were, after all, seventeen, not seven, and I couldn't believe that I was actually having this conversation. I had to control my laughter as I knew that some of them were from overseas and had only been in the country for a few years, so maybe this was lost in translation (but that was wishful thinking on my part).

I thought, how could one of them state that he stood there and watched it happen? Did he wait for the gestation period to complete? Maybe they used the wrong words, but I couldn't think of any alternatives.

I had to end the session by thanking the boys for their contributions and pointing out that any further questions not in line with the lesson would have to be taken up at the end of the day. Needless to say, I had no takers.

PROBABLY A WEEKLY SAYING

"I don't care or want to know what you're doing under the table but put both of your hands where I can see them immediately."

WHY IS IT ALWAYS ABOUT THE PENIS?

The Breaking Penis

During one of my weekly walks, I happened to be in the library when I spotted some of my level two students. One of them saw me and beckoned me over. I was initially feeling quite pleased for a number of reasons:

1. They were in the library.
2. They appeared to be working (although there's always an element of doubt in my mind).
3. They were about to ask me for advice on a sporting matter.

I was wrong all counts.

"Maxine," he said, looking me straight in the face. "Can your penis break?"

After a small pause, I said, "Yes, it can. Now, keep both hands on the table, and no you can't go to the toilet now." I was trying to cover all angles instantly.

I watched as his face registered shock, dismay, then confusion all within a matter of seconds as he listened to each of my responses. I had no idea why he chose to ask me that question or why I reacted that way. I suppose that as this came left of field, it just threw me and brought out my subconscious reactions.

The Penis Muscle

During an anatomy and physiology lesson, I was recapping on the skeletal muscles when one of my boys put his hand up to ask a question (rather too keenly, I have to say). He started shouting my name, "Maxine, Maxine," in his lovely lyrical Somalian lilt.

I turned around and hoped that it was not the usual, "Can I go to the toilet?" question. I was sure most of them needed to see the GP for their bladder problems. Anyway, back to the point. I turned round and he waved me forward with his normal big grin spread across his face. I approached, looked at him and thought, this doesn't feel right.

"Is this something that you want to ask in private?" I checked.

"No, it's ok," came the answer. "So, you're talking about skeletal muscles and the effect of exercise is that they grow and get stronger," he started then paused. I continued to look at him, and thought, oh no, I'm right, it's not a sporting question.

He then rephrased. "So, Maxine, you know when you're talking about skeletal muscles? Does that mean that if you exercise your penis, that it will grow too?"

The noise dropped. All eyes fell on me.

I looked at him and he continued to look at me with a big eager smile, eyes wide and fixed on me with no hint of embarrassment. His poise gave nothing away. Anyone would have thought that he was asking me if I took sugar in my tea.

The class waited in silence. Well, you would, wouldn't you?

Out of my mouth came, "No."

Nothing else came to mind.

Then, "But I see where you're coming from with this." I could feel the words leaving my mouth but was powerless to stop them. I didn't mean to add a sexual innuendo at this point, but luckily no one had caught on.

"It's not a skeletal muscle and has nothing to do with sport, so if you want to ask any more questions along those lines, we can talk about it later."

"Ok," he said, and returned to his work.

With that tricky situation dealt with, we moved on as if nothing untoward had ever been mentioned.

Meat and two veg

A sports injuries lesson, and I had the same students from the farting pigeon discussion.

The students were working in pairs on case studies, specifically to do with stages of injury and recovery. One pair was given a dislocated shoulder to assess and, having failed to provide an effective description of the location of the injury, I pointed to the skeleton for further guidance.

The lesson continued with its usual ebb and flow of focus and disruption. Towards the end of the class I held a few one-to-ones at the computer when Abdi pointed quietly to the skeleton. It was angled towards me. Resting in its pelvic cavity were a pair of polystyrene balls and a whiteboard pen perfectly balanced in between them.

I looked and said, "Mmm, I wonder how long they've been there?" It hadn't even crossed my mind to be offended by this or to challenge the class as to who was responsible, so I carried on giving my student his assignment feedback while retrieving the items from the skeleton to place on the desk.

Now that I'm writing this I wonder, did he do this? Was he waiting for an adverse reaction from me?

Later that evening while watching a series called Sex Education (which is based on life in a Welsh secondary school), the day came flooding back. I suddenly blurted out to my husband, "Oh my goodness. A student put a set of foam balls and a pen into the skeleton today to look like a cock 'n' balls. My head hadn't even registered what it represented. I hadn't even questioned if one of my students had put it there or how long it had been like that. I must be losing the plot, or am I getting too old to bother anymore?"

He could provide no answer.

IT HAPPENS IN THE OUTDOORS TOO

Weaselling

It was summertime and I was still trying to increase the portfolio of activities happening in the P.E department at my school (not too difficult to be honest). Well, literally nothing was happening sports-activity-wise at the end of the day. So, I was attempting to carve out my own niche and decided to team up with a couple of the Geography and Science teachers who ran the outdoor activities at the school. I was keen to give the pupils an experience of alternative types of physical activities and wanted to take them away from their immediate environment. Being a keen hill walker, I was enthused about the possibilities of sharing my love of the outdoors with them. Sheffield is perfectly placed for this, considering its close proximity to the Peak District, so all manner of activities were possible. Most of the pupils had never been on the hills, seen heather, hiked or just experienced clean countryside air, so I wanted to impress them with my knowledge of the outdoors and possibly give them something that they could continue to pursue in the future. We teamed up with the Outdoor Pursuits section of the council and arranged day activities for classes of pupils. A few of the staff had invented an activity called weaselling. This involved crawling through clusters of rocks that had formed natural spaces on top of and just below the earth. It was the perfect introduction to outdoor activities and it also encouraged participation for those pupils who were either claustrophobic or uncomfortable with the dark, as daylight could always be seen.

My husband had decided to join us on the trip (you still could in those days), and we were taken through the safety procedures before we could explore the holes. I led a small group of pupils with my husband in my group and, for the most part, the activities were going well. We led them through the rock formations with increasing levels of difficulty, to allow the pupil's confidence to grow with each successful activity.

Weaselling could be a little tricky as it involved negotiating your body around some quite tight spaces and angles. Dave decided that he was keen to go down one particular hole first and was delighted at having made his way through successfully. He did what I find most men were prone to do: give me advice on how to tackle this one. Of course, I wasn't going to listen. So down I went in, feet first.

That was mistake number one.

As soon as I descended and started to wriggle my way through a few of the bends, the reality of my error began to unfold. This particular section of rocks had quite a steep descent, so I couldn't retrace my steps to restart. Not only was there no turning room, of equal importance there was no room to make any form of physical adjustments. The hole was so narrow that my arms were held fast above my head for the duration of that activity.

I gradually realised that something was amiss in the clothing department. Nowadays, thanks to Janet Jackson, it's labelled a wardrobe malfunction. As I continued to wriggle down through the tunnel, my clothes were slowly parting company with my body. Not a problem for my shorts as they had a natural stopping point, more of a problem for my t-shirt, and more importantly, my bra. I was beginning to expose myself and could not do a thing about it. The rock formations were now even closer together and were increasingly pressing against my body on all sides. My bare skin was progressively being exposed as the pressure of the rocks increased on my body. I began to feel little cuts and nicks opening in my flesh as I continued in vain to halt the inevitable progress of exposure. Another gust of air hit my body and my face contorted, not as a result of the cold air but because my mind had just registered that I was now fully exposed. I bit my lip as I felt my breasts reacting to the chill. My bra by this point had made its way up to my armpits. Initially I thought it wouldn't be so bad as I'm wearing a sports bra and they're a bugger to get on and off at the best of times. But here I was, helpless and topless, and the rocks were undressing me with ease. I tried to wriggle to one side to create more room in an attempt to bring one arm down to my side. My thoughts were that I could at least slow down, if not halt the ensuing reveal. It was all to no avail, I had succeeded only in adding further scrapes on myself. I finally had to admit defeat and, with it, my impending embarrassment. My thoughts were, I'm going to end up topless on a school trip. How do I get out of this situation?

My mind began to work rapidly, and I started to panic and wonder who was at the business end with Dave. Luckily, I remembered that he was the first one down. I shouted down to him, hoping that the awaiting pupils and teachers waiting at the top were so concerned with the rudiments of tackling the activity that they were not listening to my shouts for help.

"Dave, can you make sure that you stand right up to the exit please. I need a little help on the way out." For once, he complied without questioning (I didn't need a domestic in public). He guarded the exit and, as I was making my way through, I started to feel warmer air on my stomach. I heard a sound that I interpreted as "Aah, now I see the problem". I then felt hands clawing up my body, pulling at my clothing to provide me with some semblance of dignity prior to my exit.

I exited the hole, clothes semi-adjusted, and much of my self-respect regained. No stories were to be told about my fight with the rocks. Surprisingly, Dave and I never had the "if only you'd followed my instructions" talk.

"MY SON'S MATE?"

Tom

A brief introduction to Tom

He was tall, self-confident, probably a little too cocky and desperately wanted to be seen as a leader.

There are always interesting challenges that often require a great deal of patience while helping others to overcome their fears, whatever the activity. This one came in the guise of my son's six-foot-four old school mate, who happened to be taking one of our Public Services courses.

We were out in the Peaks. completing the usual menu of activities: abseiling, caving, outdoor teambuilding. I was in Tom's group (the big guy) and we were about to descend into a dark cave. Helmets, head torches, and wet gear were all checked. Safety instructions were given on the cave procedures, with the instructors further reinforcing the safety points by regaling the group with a few stories of previous injuries, incidents and ultimately rescues. They ended with a warning about the changeable weather conditions, so it was imperative to pay close attention to the leaders and the surroundings. I decided to place myself in the front so that students could see when I made it through, meaning that if I could, then they could too.

We were roped up, slowly descending into the cave, and twenty minutes in all was going smoothly. Everyone's headtorches were turned on as the darkness quickly closed around us. A section of the cave was narrow so, as instructed, we had to sit on a ledge, wriggle ourselves into the furthest corner and make our way through the chimney descent (tight squeeze) in order to descend into the more open cave.

There were plenty of blind spots, so each team member had to support each other through this tricky section with suggestions for the easiest hand and footholds. Safely through, I made my way to the waiting team to admire the stalactites. I heard a low moan but I was used to this as these types of trips were all about challenging and overcoming our fears while improving team bonding. The moans increased in volume and pitch, then came the expletives. They replaced the calming atmosphere, bringing feelings of discomfort for some. I couldn't recognise the voice but immediately thought that one of the girls was in trouble. I headed back towards the direction of sound that was emanating from the area of the chimney descent. I didn't want the other students to be unnecessarily alarmed more than they needed to be. I was also attempting to prevent a rebellion among some of the more insecure ones.

As I reached the chimney, it was clear enough to hear the continued level of distress in the student's voice. I could see a pair of feet dangling from the ledge but couldn't equate the size of the feet with one of the female students: they were huge. Then it dawned on me, these feet could only belong to the last male student to complete the descent: Tom. With a quick change of how to approach this, I got up to Tom and calmly asked him about his surroundings and which bit of him was stuck (it usually just takes a little movement to readjust to the correct position.) As he started to respond, his pitch lowered, panic reduced and he was able to respond in a positive manner, rather than in his heightened tone, to express what a waste of time this was and that this was not his preferred career choice (or words to that effect). This process took some time to sort, but we eventually managed it and continued the trip with few other issues.

So why am I recalling this particular event? Later in the week my son, Aaron, said, "Mom, I saw Tom at college. He rushed over to tell me how he had to rescue you on the caving trip as you panicked and couldn't stop screaming. That he had to calm you down and help you get through a section of the cave because you were so scared and couldn't do it on your own."

Initially I was fuming. I then said to Aaron, "So how did you respond?"

"I just looked at him and said, My mom? Are you sure that was my mom?' Then Tom said, 'Yep. Never thought she'd be like that. Anyway, she was lucky coz I was there. Just thought I'd let you know.'"

Me: "Did you believe him?"

"Naw."

So I went through the story as I saw it, blow by blow.

After that, Aaron retorted, "He was always a dick at school. No change then."

I just smiled.

HOLLOWFORD: YOU LEFT YOUR SOCK...

Our college had joined forces with a number of schools across the city. We were based in Castleton at a local outdoor activity centre. I always became a little twitchy when mixing with other educational establishments. Often the rules of behaviour differ between institutions, so a middle ground is always needed and I'm rarely happy to concede. We always lay out the ground rules before we depart and reiterate them once we arrive at the accommodation.

With the activities over for the day, it was lights out at 10 pm. We explained that there should be no members of the opposite sex in the dorm rooms and that any flouting of the rules could result in parents being summoned to take their child home.

The evening was going smoothly, and the students were getting on well with each other. Some slowly slinked off to their dorms as they were tired. Gail and I were on duty and announced the fifteen-minute wind down period prior to lights out. At 11 pm, we completed our dorm checks and walked around the halls listening for voices that didn't belong in the dorms... of course we found one.

We knocked on the girl's door and asked if everything was ok. We heard shuffling and mumbling noises. "All fine here."

"Can we come in to do a head count, please? Its past lights out."

"Just a minute," came the reply.

We heard more shuffling accompanied by low voices.

"Come in."

We opened the door and saw that most girls were in their bunks with their headphones on, or they were just chatting. We counted.

"There are only seven of you."

"Yes, Mel's in the bathroom."

"Right, can you make sure that as soon as she's back that the lights are out, please."

"No problem. Night."

We left the dorm. By then we had figured out what the score was, but we were not allowed to enter the bathroom. Gail suggested that we check on the boy's dorm two doors down. Again, we hear noises, but not much. We repeated our entry requests. Another headcount and we realised that, again, one person was missing. "Where's Mark?" They looked at us and shrugged their shoulders, no one was willing to spill the beans.

We thanked them and left.

We now had two students missing, it was past 11 pm and we suspected that we knew where they were. We needed to find them so decided on a plan of attack. One quick staff conference later and we found ourselves knocking on the two dorm rooms at midnight. Students emerged, some bleary-eyed, some annoyed at being disturbed from their conversations, some from their sleep. We lined them up and completed a roll call. Mel had now reappeared.

"Are you ok, Mel?" I asked, wanting to have some eye contact with her to see if I could read her face.

She looked straight at me with a "Yes thanks."

I'd read nothing.

Gail went into the girl's dorm to check but came out alone. The boys were lined up. Another head count, and there was still one missing: Mark. There was a notable shift among the girls. Gail again searched the dorm and again emerged empty handed.

"Ok," she says. "We have a very serious problem. Mark is still missing, and no one seems to know where he is. Let me remind you of an incident that has happened previously resulting in the police, ambulance and parents being called. There was a student who decided that the rules were not for him and, during the late-night check-up, decided to jump out of the girl's dorm window in order to get back to his dorm. Only he misjudged the height, broke his ankle and stayed there most of the night. When he was eventually found, he was also suffering from mild hypothermia. Need I go on? I can assure you that his parents were not too pleased to receive a call at 3 am, asking them to go to the hospital to be with their child. Are you getting the picture?"

They were all looking at their feet, no one was willing to give him up. We gave them five minutes before we said he would officially be a missing person and we would have to inform the police. All eyes slowly turned to the left down the corridor; Mark was timidly tiptoeing towards the boy's line. The staff faced him in unison. No words were said. He mumbled, "I needed the bathroom and ours was occupied so I used the one in the hallway. I didn't know that you were looking for me, or I'd have come out sooner."

Was that nervous sweat or rain on his face? I thought, Mmm his hair and clothes look a little damp too. A quick scan and I also noted that he had one sock missing. I nudged Gail. She'd noticed this too and I excused myself, saying there was somewhere I needed to be. I quickly walked past him, dipped my eyes to note the mud trail of footprints and sock-prints leading to the outside. I followed the trail and, sure enough, there was the missing sock, in between the boy's and girl's room.

On my return, they'd dismissed the others and were interviewing Mark in another room. I walked in and presented them with the sock. We waited and his mouth dropped open but no words came out as he knew he'd been caught. All I asked was, "When Gail and I came into the girl's dorm, were you in the bathroom with Mel?" I already knew the answer.

He whispered, "Yes," and continued to mumble that he panicked when we knocked on the door so ran into the bathroom when Mel was coming out. When it was safe, he escaped out of the window and couldn't get into the boy's room as they had no idea that he was there, so he then had to walk around the building and hadn't realised that he'd lost his sock until it was too late. He reiterated how sorry he was for the inconvenience caused and that it was his fault alone.

His staff were left to make the decision on what should happen to him. It's never an easy solution as there were lots of people involved. Needless to say, the next morning his behaviour was too upbeat and, as far as I was concerned, he certainly hadn't eaten enough humble pie. Whether he learned his lesson, I'll never know.

DEBBIE THE NEWBIE

The science block was at the other end of the school and overlooked the school courtyard. Bored pupils could hail their mates from the second floor or hold spitting competitions out of the teacher's eye shot; the bigger and greener, the better the prize (guess the targets).

Debbie was usually very poised and calm and carried herself with ease. Today she came running down the corridor all flustered and red-faced. I could see the tears in her eyes and quickly found her somewhere quiet, giving her a moment to calm herself down and explain her situation. She then began.

"I was in the middle of an experiment and the pupils were around the table watching me. As usual, Darren was getting most of the attention and started to stand on the table. I told him to get down, but he complained that he couldn't see. So, I told him to come round to the front."

At this point, I need to explain that Darren was rather a small child, with any sign of pending maturation in the far distance, and for some reason his satchel was permanently ensconced on his back.

"Darren took objection to what he thought was a jab at his lack of height and told me that he was bored with the lesson and that his mates were outside, so he was going to jump out the window. So, I thought I'd call his bluff and told him to go on and jump."

"And?" I asked. "What happened?"

"He jumped," she said.

" You're on the second floor!" I retorted. "And" (to stretch the point even further) "the windows have restricted openings."

"He's small, remember," she said.

I didn't know what to think, so asked, "What happened then?"

"He ran off with his satchel still on his back."

I stood there looking at her and visualised the look on her face as she watched helplessly as Darren jumped on the table, wriggled through the window with his satchel on his back and flew (jumped) to his freedom.

"Well, that's ok then, no harm done," was the only reply I could think of.

UMRA (MAT'S STORY)

Umra

A brief introduction to Umra.

He was comedy value and probably did not realise the extent of this. He had an interesting background as he had been in the country for a few years so his grasp of the language and his interpretations would often result in a surprised look on our faces or outbursts of laughter. He lacked self-confidence but was supported well by his peers who protected him fiercely.

We were completing our practical session as Umra came over to me, prodding his stomach and complaining of stomach ache. He sometimes got his words mixed up, possibly while translating from his native tongue to English. I wanted to get more of an idea of what type of pain it was. I don't think he said the following on purpose as it was with a very straight face, or maybe he had heard this expression from someone.

"Well," he said, "it feels like I'm shitting my organs out. A number two."

"Oh my goodness. Did anyone hear?"

"Other students were nearby but somehow missed it." I had to turn around and cracked up laughing. He just stood there holding his side, not knowing what I was laughing about. You can't write this stuff"

"True," I replied.

STRICTLY COME DANCING THIS AINT

There were often times when the sports students were joined by students from other courses to complete a smaller qualification. This year for some reason had a complement of dance students. Together, they were being taught a unit on coaching. Each student had to be assessed while coaching a practical session. The dance students all defaulted to their main subjects as their vehicle. Amanda implemented the step bench to integrate the world of sport and dance, and to provide a semblance of familiarity for the boys. I knew that this would be entertaining, I just had no idea how much.

The place was EISS (English Institute of Sport Sheffield). We had the pleasure of being a few handshakes away from some of the country's elite athletes and coaches and were often able to watch and make notes on the high-level coaching and performance taking place. This was not to be reciprocated though, particularly on this occasion.

The session began without music to quickly assess the classes basic movement skills. The boys were placed in rows behind the benches, with the remainder of the dance students interspersed to help them with the rhythm. Amanda used the tried and tested method of a basic step touch to the side. So far so good... well ok, but not impressive (remember, this was the simple section). She then added music.

That was mistake number one. Well, I was really hoping that the lesson could develop beyond this, but my hopes had already begun to dwindle.

Support was given by counting the steps in time to the music. A nice and easy step touch, step touch, one, two, three, four, repeat. One of the problems was the actual counting (up to four) in conjunction with the side stepping.

"Start off on your right foot."

"The other right foot, please."

Shauna tapped Ryan's leg to provide some physical stimulus.

She then tapped Warren's.

Scott thought he's got it, you could see the visible relief on his face.

Increasing grunts of frustration ricocheted around the sports hall from Ryan, Ben and Warren as they continued to look at their feet, checking their location and movement of their right and left feet to see if it matched their peers. This was quickly followed by, "Oh my God, I've got to move to the other right. Man I can't get this."

Amanda continued to encourage and praise from the front and decided to take it up a notch and tell them that it would all feel easier in the next section, as their coordination would continue to improve. She asked them to stop while she demonstrated the next move, which included using the step bench.

"All you're doing is transferring your weight onto the box. Instead of step touch to the side, step onto the box with a wide stance, left, right, then off the box to a narrow position."

I watched as the level of intensity increased yet another notch, as the boys now had to attempt to add equipment into their already challenging routine. Maybe they'd peaked at walking forwards and backwards, I thought. Feet stumbled onto benches, then teetered off them; they clashed, scraped shins and stepped in when they should have been stepping out. Maybe they really needed L and R written on their trainers.

Change of plan number two. Amanda instructed, "Please look up and follow my direction."

She pointed to the left, then to the right, while counting.

"Ryan, look at me, and try not to move forward when you do."

"Scott, when I go forward, you do too, it's supposed to be mirror image."

A car crash was building up.

Ryan began to stomp about, all six-foot-four of him.

Ben? Well, I can't begin to explain what was happening there.

They clashed in the middle. Ryan's size twelve feet on Bens size nines.

I remembered that I also had to record the lesson as the evidence would be needed for external verification. However, the familiar feelings of laughter began to take shape internally. My shoulders began to shake and my stomach tensed as I fought to maintain some basic level of control, but knew that this battle was already lost. My stomach began to ache as I tried in vain to quell the sound that was building up. Involuntarily yelps of laughter spilled through my mouth. I looked at the camera and realised this was still being recorded, but what could I do? Luckily, the sports hall had a dividing curtain so I could at least physically hide my emotions, but I had to keep recording. I left the camera running and collapsed, trying in vain to stifle my laughter by covering my mouth with the curtains. Tears were rolling down my face and my cheeks and abs hurt while I was desperately attempting to hold it all in.

I felt the girl's pain.

I heard Amanda's voice again and this time I sensed her despair.

"The next the section is where you can improvise. Work in pairs to produce some form of dance movement for the next eight counts." (She was defeated).

I eventually stuck my head around the curtains. No words could ever describe the carnage. They managed the eight counts. Just. There appeared to be no relationship between the physical movements and the music. Who was working with whom? It was almost impossible to decipher. As for the timing? What timing. Oh my goodness. Were they trying to work in synchro with each other? To the music? Offbeat/on the beat? All or none of the above? They just appeared to be very red-faced, frustrated young men who had allowed a few young women to publicly humiliate them in the name of art.

After a total of thirty minutes, even with the extensive help, the girls realised that there really was little hope.

Amanda had the last laugh though, as she asked each group to add their improvised sections to the opening steps that they had learned and then demonstrate them to the class to show some progression. Well, when I said learned and demonstrate, these were very loose descriptive terms. They could demonstrate something, it could never be described as learned.

It was torturous to watch. This was my cue to again resume my position behind the curtain and howl with laughter. By this point, I'd given up any hope of decorum. I regained sufficient composure to retake my position behind the camera, only to see the boys jump on the boxes in unison, thrust their arms in the air and shout, "Offside."

I was exhausted. This class had made my day, if not my year.

The next lesson, the girls needed feedback to help with their coaching analysis. Luckily for them, I still had the recordings. The atmosphere was a mix of anticipation (the boys) and gloom (the girls). I couldn't believe that the boys still clung to the idea that they were "not too shabby." I watched their faces as they recognised each other, then witnessed the changes. The transformation was a picture, the upturned lips quickly dropped, their mouths hung open and a head hit the desk. They now understood why I had to keep on disappearing... and that laughter; I wasn't holding anything back! With the evidence presented to them, they could no longer deny their inability to coordinate the most simplistic of movements. I had nothing more I say.

BEN: BADMINTON AND THOSE SAUSAGE ROLLS

Ben

A brief introduction to Ben.

Height wise, Ben was unfortunate enough to be born in the wrong year. It was not that he was particularly short, it was more that his peers happened to be quite tall. Combine that with his naturally slim stature, and his typically British posture; he gave the appearance of being much shorter and frailer than his five-foot nine-inch height. allowed

Mishaps always seemed to occur when Ben was around; he was always the recipient of these and would often enter the class and begin his sentences with: 'Guess what happened to me today lads?"

The following story is a typical example

The Sausage Rolls

Monday morning. No one wanted to be in college, not the students, not me. It was the day of the energy systems lesson, never an easy subject. The students piled in and took their places. The register was taken, Ben was missing, which was strange as he was never usually absent. "Scott, did you see Ben this weekend? Was he ok? Is he coming in?"

"I'm glad you asked me that, as a funny thing happened at Morrisons' on Saturday." Scott responded, Something amusing was always happening to Ben, so I was interested to hear what Scott had to say. He were asked by his manager to go t't freezer to fetch sausage rolls as they were running low on't shelves. Another member of staff thought that the door had been accidentally left open, so he shut it. Meanwhile, Ben were in there fetching rolls up a ladder, he toppled o'er, sausage rolls landed on his head. It were a full un you know, a full tray. Knocked him out cold. He lay there for ages before anyone found him. They had to cart him off t' 'ospital."

Suffice it to say, that was not the answer I expected. I wasn't sure how to react and the other students were howling with laughter. I looked at Scott and realised that there might be a few exaggerated points but, essentially, he was telling the truth. My immediate concern was of the company's health and safety policies and of the investigations that would probably be needed as it sounded as though he had had some level of concussion.

All some students said was " Well that'll knock some sense into im."

Later on that day, I phoned home to ensure that he was ok. His mom answered, "It could only happen to Ben. Knocked him out cold, they did".

It was 3 weeks before Ben returned to college.

Twelve years later I messaged Ben to ask him if he minded sharing the story. He was more than happy to.

Below is his recollection.

"Basically, I were knocked out int freezer by an estimated weight of sixteen stone worth of frozen foods. Luckily someone found me otherwise I would have froze to death. I were off college for around three week as it were a fairly serious head injury.

The gag about me came into place when lads at college found out that the majority of food were sausage rowls. When I came back t' college the big screen int lobby area int college ad a video of a stick man with me head on it and a sausage roll chasing me then hitting me on head. I've never eaten a sausage roll since lol."

Badminton

There are fundamental skills that sport staff expect students to have developed, particularly if they've chosen to study the subject at this level. In particular when teaching a practical lesson, staff would expect sports students to have well-developed or at least reasonable coordination skills. Typically the boys tend to turn up to our classes with the strange preconceived notion that the course is all about football, and that of course they hold the requisite skills to succeed.

This lesson wasn't football though. It was the first taught badminton session of the term, so I was keeping it was nice and simple. I had prepared a lesson on the overhead clear as the main taught skill.

The students paired up, and I demonstrated the actions before setting them off on their tasks. I walked round to correct and encourage, then stopped to watch two of the students as something unusual seemed to be happening. Ryan was supposed to be completing his overhead clear and appeared to be motionless. I stood behind him and my eyes then turned to Ben, his partner. The racket went back then forward, the shuttlecock was thrown into the air, then came down again, no connection was made. This happened time and time again and I witnessed Ben's mounting frustration. I'd never witnessed this before; he was totally unable to connect the shuttlecock with his racket.

I remained still while I thought about how to overcome this. Ryan was becoming increasingly annoyed as he had nothing to do. His shouts of encouragement and advice quickly took on an aggressive tone and as a result, Ben's frustration at his inability to hit the shuttlecock became synchronised with Ryan's emotions.

Changes were needed imminently to avoid additional attention to Ben. Ryan was quickly placed in another group; I then worked with Ben on the fundamentals. It still wasn't easy. At one point I thought I was going to have to resort to buying a racket with a large head to provide some modicum of success. At that time, even with a whiff of air between racket and shuttlecock, success was very limited.

Each week Ben stressed about the lesson to the point of feigning illness. I had to ensure that he was at the end of the court to provide special coaching without the additional attention. It took almost a term for us to see the impact, but that look on his face was worth it.

WHY CAN'T I HAVE MY OWN PLACE?

Bejal

A brief introduction to Bejal.

He is an amateur boxer and wants to pursue it professionally; he comes from quite a traditional Muslim/Iranian family. He is very polite and holds particular views regarding the status of men and women in society. When questioned about some of his comments he often looks at me and can't understand why I'm making an issue of it. That's just how it is where he comes from.

I teach level two students (the equivalent of four GCSE's). Some of them have ambitions to study at level three then onto university, whereas others want to go directly into the world of work. It can therefore be seen as a stepping stone towards university or, alternatively, another year of figuring out their career paths. Bejal belonged to the former group. I knew of his ambitions but just couldn't work out his motivation for his subject choice at times. I also couldn't work out whether he disliked women in general, me in particular, or both.

He was often telling me that men should be the bread winners and women belonged at home looking after the house, which he would say with sincerity and no malice. I'm not even sure if he recognised me as a woman, as when I questioned him he would always say, "Well, you're different."

I didn't bother to ask what he meant by that. Bejal gained his level two and changed subjects for his level three course. I would often chat to him around college, exchanging small talk to see how he was doing.

One day Bejal knocked on my office door. I ushered him in and asked what I could do for him. He explained that I needed to find him somewhere to live as he needed to live independently of his family. Alarm bells rang as I envisaged a child protection situation unfolding, so I gently began to question him.

"Has someone assaulted you?"

"No."

"Were you being bullied?"

"No."

My probing questions were all returned with negative answers.

Ok, I thought, lets tackle this from another angle. I knew that he was a keen boxer, so I decided to ask about this.

"I'm not going anymore," he replied.

I wasn't expecting that. He'd often talked about moving onto cage fighting.

"I've fallen out with my dad, he's cruel."

But that was all that I could get from him, except that college had found one of his friends a flat so it was therefore his right to get one too. I saw where this was going and remembered his comments from the previous year, so I thought I'd dig a little deeper.

"If you got a flat where would the finance come from?"

"The council."

Ok, I thought.

"What about shopping and cooking? How will you manage that?"

"Well, before I get a wife, some woman from the council will come and do that, won't they?"

He really believed his own story.

"So, some woman from the council will do your shopping, cooking, cleaning and ironing for you, is that right?"

"Yes."

There was such assurance in his voice that I knew that he believed that this was a probability. I couldn't get any further with his issues so told him I'd look into it.

I invited his father in with his sister as I thought I might need an interpreter. I didn't trust how my student might interpret his father's words and was still unsure of his home situation.

We were all in the room. I was aware that this could be a delicate situation, so I had to make sure that I was in control. I asked Bejal to explain his side of the story. He began by saying that his father wanted to know where he was when he came in late at night and what he was spending his money on when he continued to ask for money. He didn't see why he should tell him. He needed his own space.

I couldn't believe my ears. Was that what this was all about, a strike for his independence? His father just sat there with his head bowed.

I asked his father for his side of the story. It transpired that his son had no respect for his father and demanded money but wouldn't tell his father what it was for. It had come to the point that he would rather his son left his house than be disrespectful to him. It turns out that his father spoke perfect English and didn't need an interpreter, but his sister interjected by saying that her brother was spoiled at home and didn't do anything around the house. She explained that when Bejal got home, his dinner is put on the table and, when he is finished, his plate is removed and washed up by someone else.

Bejal's words from the previous year came back to me as I could now see where his attitude about women came from; it was his personal experience, his norm.

I looked at Bejal and said to him that as a parent myself I would react the same as his dad. I would be putting curfews in place and demanding to know what he was spending his money on. I repeated what his sister had said about being spoilt, but also went on to say that getting his own place, when the time was right, would be an amazing experience. In the meantime, I suggested he take a few lessons from his mom and sister and learn some of the domestic tasks in order to become independent and less reliant on others for help.

His father and sister thanked me for my time and Bejal just smiled at me. Well, that's my interpretation.

BERLIN: THE LLAMA STORY AND FARTS...

I wasn't particularly excited about the day of the zoo trip, as I felt that there were lots of other cultural options that we could explore. However, we had let the students choose some of the activities, so we had to comply. The students were given their allocated two tickets: one for the aquarium and the other for the remainder of the zoo. They were then given the rendezvous time and place, which presented the perfect opportunity for me, Ian, Andy and Ash, the staff members to be student-less for a little while.

As we entered the aquarium, we were joined by another student who appeared a little perturbed. He approached Ian, one of the party leaders, and told us that another student, Alex, had lost his ticket and needed our help. We took in the information and I'm sure we all had the same thoughts: if we rescue him, we would be stuck with him for the rest of the afternoon, he was a little needy and didn't necessarily respond to the usual teacher clues that we all defer to when we wanted to be left alone. Our teacher game face would have to be reinstated and that would be the end of our adult conversations.

Ian had to vouch for Alex at the entrance and Alex, true to form, was so grateful for the rescue that he attached himself to us for the rest of the day. Having looked at a variety of fish, then the apes, he spouted, "Why are zebras here? They don't belong in Berlin?"

"Neither do the rest of the animals," I retorted

Alex had a tendency to embellish conversations and could capture you for an inordinate amount of time if you weren't careful. Andy (staff) hated snakes and gave reference to watching a snake video when young.

Alex: "So, Andy, have you ever experienced taming anacondas?" That was it, he'd captured Andy's attention, and we found our get out of jail card. We glanced at each other and realised that the opportunity was staring us in the face. Together, myself, Ian and Ash immediately synchronised the speed of our pace to the point where we were just out of earshot to be unable to respond to any ensuing conversation, leaving Andy to entertain Alex. (Sorry Andy)

Andy: "Whatever made you say that?"

No reply.

Alex: "Have you heard the Llama Song?"

Andy: "You've got me. If I said I have, would it stop you from singing it?"

He sang it anyway.

Later on that evening, when recalling the conversation, Andy was quick to point out how he distinctly remembers hearing a subtle but audible involuntary laugh from Ash when Alex asked the llama question. and all he could think was "Do I make the very obvious but very inappropriate large penis innuendo? What is he even talking about? Is he aware that he's setting me up for that? What is happening" My only response was Andy: "Whatever made you say that?"

***

It was the penultimate day of our trip and Ian announced that everyone needed to go retro and take photos with their peers from photo booths across the city. The group rose to the challenge and were squeezing into booths to mark the occasion for our trip scrapbook. I was asked to squeeze into a booth with two of the students, so we all squashed in together. Sarah, who had behaved impeccably all week, had previously announced that she had fallen in love with the city so much that she was going to come and study here (adding that if she nabbed a

German husband on the way that wouldn't be too bad either).

While in the booth, she made a small announcement "I'm going to fart."

Her tone was flat, as if she was asking me to shuffle over in order to get her in the shot.

As a teacher, when in the class there are a few ways to tackle this: ignore it, play it down or talk about bodily functions in an attempt to embarrass the culprit. None of these ideas were going to work here.

I thought this announcement was for the camera shot but, no, she happened to be sitting on Jerim's knee. It had happened and it was an SBD (Silent but Deadly). The whiff wafted towards our noses and the small enclosed space really didn't help.

My nostrils flared and I tried holding my breath but almost collapsed with the smell.

Sarah just sat and looked at us.

"What's the problem?" she said. I came to the conclusion long ago that I'm more of a tomboy than a lady and I don't have a problem with it. I hang out with boys mostly so have learned to embrace my windiness."

No more could be said except to hold my breath for the photo shoot and scramble out of the booth to gasp for clean air.

I'm still stunned when I see her. How can someone who looks so delicate produce something so deadly?

THAT SPANISH RESIDENTIAL (DIFFERENT TIMES)

It was the time when educational funding was a plenty. Manufacturing jobs were reducing so the college had taken on students from the local steel works, and some of these took the opportunity to study sport. The class was a mix of fresh wet behind the ears sixteen-year-olds and almost middle-aged men mid-thirties and over. The annual trip to Spain was booked so we had an interesting mix of staff and students. On arrival at the hotel, after completion of the group check in, the trip organiser, John, disappeared. He happened to have a very good grasp of Spanish; we were later to discover that his absence coincided with that of the local female interpreter who we had assumed was employed to be in our company for the duration of the trip.

There appeared to be no instructions or restrictions given to the party; they were therefore left to fend for themselves for the evening. On the first night, two of the staff members Tom and Jayne, decided that they would climb the mountain track, with Tom in his flip-flops. They insisted that they could ascend to the cliff top and return before dark. Well of course they couldn't and they didn't.

After waiting a few hours and seeing no sign of them, the Spanish outdoor activity staff and some of the more mature students eventually had to rescue them. They wouldn't admit that they'd got lost and instead insisted that they'd lost all track of time while pondering the beauty of the Spanish fauna and flora.

This set the tone for the trip. The students rolled in at any time and it was a little difficult to set a curfew considering the age differences. Jayne was continually being summoned by the hotel owner and told off for the group's tardiness (the lead organiser was still nowhere to be found). So the older students took the younger students under their wing.

One morning at the hotel, one of the staff noted that Wayne, one of the sixteen-year-olds, was missing. His peers freely admitted that they'd left him at the fun fare. As he was drunk, they'd paid the staff to give him extra rides. Exasperated by this, Jayne sent them off to retrieve him. He was still there on a ride, fast asleep.

***

It was the late eighties and, for those of you in the know, the "Curly Perm" was popular with black males and females alike. If you're still in need of further education, then the Jerry Curl scene from the film Coming to America is a perfect example. Jayne was still receiving complaints from the hotel owner, this time because of the excessive gel on some of the students pillows. She had no idea what they meant, so went to talk to the boys one morning in their room. Having knocked on the door a few times and hearing no reply, she decided that she would enter. The door opened easily and she popped her head round to see the two boys lying face down on the beds with carrier bags over their heads. She panicked and immediately thought that they had been experimenting sexually and had asphyxiated. On closer inspection, and having checked that they were still breathing, she realised that the bags were only covering their hair and not their faces, therefore protecting the pillows from the gel. After breathing a sigh of relief, she then inhaled, and alcohol fumes hit her nostrils. They were probably still intoxicated from the previous night. True to form, she woke them up. How were they going to get out of this one?

Jayne's room was on the ground floor, strategically placed to enable her to react quickly to the comings and goings of both students and staff. This was not really paying off and she was kept awake by noises in the room above. She remained alert and left it a little while, in the hope that they would settle, but they didn't. There was no other solution than to investigate the noise and put an end to it. Her previous experience of walking in on the boys was still lodged in her brain and she recalled that the door didn't squeak, which was important because the element of surprise was needed. However, it wasn't the surprise that she was expecting, as the boys managed to surprise her. Her eyes beheld two black bottoms going up and down in tandem, accompanied by two white bodies underneath. Also, the beds were pushed together (why?). She didn't know what to do.

"I'll give you thirty seconds to sort yourselves out," was all she could muster. She saw the girls, noted that they looked local and asked them for the name of their school, wondering what she would be telling their parents. She needed to think this through. The trip had so far been a disaster from start to finish.

Later in the day, the same students should have been taking part in outdoor activities. Jayne spotted the boys, sitting on benches. On enquiring why they were there, they dully responded, "Waiting for the girls."

"Why?"

"Trying to sort out the morning after pill."

At this point Jayne could withhold her rage no longer.

"You mean to tell me that you didn't even put a jacket on it? Turn round. See that sign? It's a Catholic country. Good luck."

With that off her chest, she left them to stew.

***

It was the last morning of an eventful residential and time for a little sun-worshipping prior to the long coach trip home. Jayne lay on her front in a secluded bay and decided to undo her bikini top. A scream was heard and she sprang up, leaving her bikini top firmly embedded in the sand. She looked up and before she could strategically place her hands in front of her, a flash went off. Paul (staff) was standing there grinning from ear to ear. There were no convivial exchanges of words to be had that day. Weeks later, she was presented with that shot, nicely framed too. The negative remained with the owner.

Later, everyone was packed and on the coach. John magically reappeared aptly dressed in a union jack tie and matching shorts. Feeble excuses were made for his lack of presence on the trip; he mumbled something about needing to continue the liaisons to ensure that everything ran smoothly for the trip's duration . No one quite knew how to respond... to his outfit or his speech. He was now ready though to resume his place at the helm. As the coach approached the border, he insisted on aiding the smooth transition by liaising with border patrol. Afterall, he was the only one equipped to handle such matters as he had previously worked with Customs (as he constantly told us). Success: not only had he managed to get everyone taken off the coach, the border staff then followed this up with a two-hour coach search. The vitriol directed in his direction gave him no choice but to self-isolate for the remainder of the journey. It was a very long journey home.

THE OFSTED CALL 2014

Anthropomorphic

"...resembling or made to resemble a human form..."

https://www.dictionary.com

A difficult one to get your tongue around.

(Word of the day)

Mark

A brief introduction to Mark

He's tall, gangly, a little uncoordinated and ungainly due to his continued growth spurts, he was blond and very polite. He would always say please, thank you and excuse me and was generally a pleasure to teach. He got on well with his peers and needed a little persuasion to respond verbally in the class but wanted to do well in his chosen field.

The Ofsted (Office for Standards in Education) inspection is either an opportunity to celebrate institutional improvements or to reflect on what could have been. Either way, we find different coping mechanisms to get through the process. The email lands in your inbox, followed up with an emergency meeting, and the principal says, "Please don't stay all weekend, you need your rest for Monday."

You know that means see you Saturday or Sunday.

The following Tuesday morning, I was teaching my usual level two class. They were generally nonproblematic and easy to teach and manage.

Not this time.

Rarely in my career have I ever needed to be rescued. In my educational establishment, I tended to be the rescuer.

The morning's lesson was fine, the students were aware that there were inspectors in the building and that they might venture into the class, listen, write notes, look at their work and possibly ask questions. They were used to this. When no inspector arrived, there was always either a tinge of regret (when the lessons went well) or of relief (not quite so well.) Today, my thoughts were in the former camp. One down, one to go. After lunch, the class returned. The door was open and as usual I gave a quick recap of the morning's lesson. A quick headcount before the register: all here. I turned to the wipe board to add some notes when, out of the corner of my eye I saw movement, followed by a crash, a sliding sound, shouting, swearing then stifled moans. I turned again, only to spot that in the furthest corner of the classroom, Mark had his hands firmly wrapped around Tom's neck. With his body strewn across two desks, three other students were desperately trying to unravel the carnage that had quickly developed. They had totally blocked off one section of the room. The remaining students sat firmly in their chairs, shocked and unsure of how to react.

I had to act immediately, the student nearest the door was directed to the staffroom to summon the duty manager. I then attempted to wade through the collapsed desks and flailing arms and legs of the supporting students before I could even get to Mark.

This normally placid student was now behaving like a rabid dog. Some of his peers had managed to loosen his grip and continued to hold him back. His rants were indecipherable, as he constantly lurched forward in his desperation to resume his strangle hold. I started to do the only thing possible: assert my presence and hope for the best.

Within two minutes not one but three managers had arrived. They momentarily paused, expressed their disbelief when they realised that it was me leading the class, then sprang into action.

Between us, we managed to control the situation. As per procedure, the two boys were separated and placed in different rooms with individual members of staff monitoring them. I was advised to take five minutes to regroup while another member of staff sat with my class.

I had no idea why that had happened, but we were still mid-inspection and I needed to rescue the lesson quickly. The idea of an inspector walking through the door at that moment would have brought me to my knees.

I managed to complete the lesson with half of the class still dazed and the other half slowly coming down from their adrenaline rush. Needless to say, very little learning took place.

Thankfully, no inspector arrived.

The lesson ended and I asked a few of the students to stay behind so I could thank them for supporting Tom and also to try get the backstory before they had the chance to merge fact with fiction.

Apparently, Mark was under the impression that Tom had been talking about him behind his back, so he asked his peers about it at lunchtime. They claimed that nothing was said. He was obviously unsatisfied with the answers given and became increasingly wound up over lunch while out in the local area. They told him that they were returning to college for my lesson, but he said that he was staying put. They had hoped that he would calm down and didn't feel the need to inform me. They only realised how bad it was when he came running into the class diving across the desk towards Tom.

In my error, I had also miscalculated the class numbers and had not yet taken the register, so had failed to note his absence.

Having later reviewed the video evidence, it was clear to see Mark sprinting through the college doors and up the steps towards my class. No one was present to stop this. As there is no CCTV in my class, the footage ended there and, of course, the story continued to unfold during my lesson.

He was immediately suspended pending an investigation, then required to attend a final stage Disciplinary Panel with his dad.

The result of the eventual Disciplinary Panel was permanent exclusion from college. Later that week, his father came into college to present me with a handwritten note from his son. He was most apologetic for his behaviour and couldn't understand what had got into him. We both agreed that this was extreme and totally out of character. I accepted the apology and stated that he was usually a pleasure to teach. I provided further advice on ways forward post the disciplinary outcome. His father left feeling grateful.

Mark's letter went on to make further apologies for his behaviour and stated that he had been wound up since the beginning of the week and just saw red that day. He said that he was determined not to listen to the advice of anyone in his class and that he had made up his mind to get his own back for the alleged rumours started by Tom. He thought that the class were all on Tom's side too, so he ran all the way from Firth Park to have it out with him. By the time he got through the college doors, he admitted to being totally out of control and just couldn't stop himself but was really sorry for disrespecting me and the class. Apology accepted.

WRONG ADDRESS

A student was given her placement address to visit on Halifax Road. Her father took her to Halifax. On his return he said, "I don't think she'll be going. It's too far."

She had missed a vital section of the address. Sheffield.

THE MOTHER/DAUGHTER PROSTITUTES

BASICS (British Association of Sport in Colleges) was made up of annual regional knock-out sports tournaments, culminating in a residential weekend for the regional winners in England. Once the regional winners had been decided, each institution then had to raise the funds required for the overall competitions. Included in fundraising costs was the kit, transport, and accommodation. Each year, the annual competition was hosted by a different region. This year, the North East region were the hosts, with Ashington as the chosen area. Our lead organiser, Jayne, had arranged for the team to stay at the Rex Hotel in Whitely Bay, chosen for its seclusion and the fact it could exclusively house our entire team. The usual health and safety talks were given, with a reminder to students that they were representing the college and should any shenanigans occur there would be no hesitation to drive them to the train station and send them home.

Convinced that the message was received and understood, the students were sent to unpack. We were a fifty-strong team covering a multitude of sports that year, so there was plenty of camaraderie among us all. Tom's birthday happened to fall that weekend; he was a quiet, lovely, introverted member of the badminton team and he would have been happy to continue to merge into the background and celebrate unnoticed. However, word spread of his impending birthday, so the team decided to have a whip round and hold a disco downstairs in the hotel. This way we could contain everything and manage any situation as they arose.

It was all going rather well... too well really. The students were happily dancing or chatting, and staff saw this as the perfect opportunity to get a swift pint in (with a few key members choosing not to imbibe should they need to intervene). During her walk around, Jayne had got wind of some unexpected information; she quickly alerted Jake, another staff member, and together they scanned the room for any issues. In our midst were a few people that just didn't quite fit the bill of sporting student or attending staff.

Some of the sports team had found out that Tom was still a virgin and wanted to give him a birthday that he'd never forget. They'd had a secret whip round and bought him... let's say an alternative present. It was a mother and daughter pairing. He was to receive a "double whammy" from this "special" pair of sex workers. A few students were placed at the bar on the lookout for the signal to entice the as yet unaware Tom to an allocated location for his birthday initiation. Jayne homed in on the approaching women but hadn't spotted that their minders were also in tow. As the women headed for the bar, Jayne intercepted them with a swift, "Sorry, there's none a that business 'ere. These are minors and in our charge." They stopped in their tracks. After much eyeballing, and no doubt waiting for their minders to step in, they admitted defeat, made a U-turn and headed for the nearest exit. Having successfully dismissed the sex workers, Jayne turned her eyes towards the boys at the bar, totally unaware of the developing situation behind her. She proceeded to give the boys a good tongue-lashing, but despite this they were still unfazed and had the audacity to demand a full refund for the unused services.

Jake had noted the confrontation between the women from an adjacent side of the room. He'd also spotted two men quickly approaching them and realised that the situation could swiftly get out of hand. Without too much thought, he played the superhero and completed a pincer move on them before they could proceed any further. A small fracas then developed between them.

The next morning at breakfast, Jake sheepishly appeared. He slinked into his seat, sporting a fresh black eye. When he opened his mouth to explain to the rest of the staff, there was a notable gap where two teeth were originally. The staff say nothing. The message swiftly rushed round the breakfast hall. One student had the audacity to remind him of "the talk," and said asked "So, when's your train, Jake?"

BET HE DOESN'T REMEMBER THAT!

It was around the year 2000 and the place was Meadowhall, Yorkshire's first out-of-town shopping centre. A new Sainsburys had opened inside. So, like the rest of the local population (or so it seemed), myself and Dave (husband) had travelled to the north of the city to check it out ,we were obviously trying to see if it was any different from the Sainsburys nearer to us. Where am I going with this, you may ask? While there, a man in his early thirties rushed up to us.

"It's Miss err... Miss, oh I can't remember your name."

He seemed frustrated. We stood there in front of him, not bothering to ask his name. My mind began to whirl. He's calling me Miss, so he is not someone that I've taught recently, he must be from my first teaching job. I therefore narrowed it down to 1983-85. By then, having taught for up to seventeen years, the student's names as well as the years of teaching had begun to blur.

My trick to try regain some semblance of information about a previous student is to ask them who else was in their class or year, then make general chit chat until they somehow disclose their name. I wasn't given any time to go through my usual routine though, as he suddenly spouted, "I'll go and ask Pamela."

Pamela was working on the tills at the time and for some reason I had always remembered who she was.

We carried on shopping, then after about ten minutes he returned.

"It's Miss Blake."

"Oh, hello again."

I was looking at this man who was tall (about six foot four) and slim, when it dawned on me. "Oh, you were at school with Carl, Pamela, Sharon and Tracy," I said.

Small chat then ensued for about ten minutes. Afterwards, we said our goodbyes as Dave remained at my side, slightly disinterested. Then it dawned on me.

Oh my God, I really do remember him.

That's when the story spilled out to my husband. You know when something so bad happens that it gets buried deeply and forgotten? Well, this was one of those.

I was teaching P.E. in the sports hall. To be more specific, I was teaching trampolining to the aforementioned group. The pupils around the trampoline had been taught how to spot correctly so they knew how to put their hands up if a pupil was going off centre, in order to gently guide them back to the centre of the trampoline. Things were going smoothly and my former pupil, Ahmed, was on the trampoline with his back to me (try not to let your minds race too far ahead to guess the storyline: it's probably not what you're thinking). Suddenly, at the far side two of the girls literally fell to the floor in a state of distress (Tracy and Sharon actually). He hadn't bounced off-centre so there was no safety issue here. I decided to walk round to help them and see what the problem was.

I looked at them and they looked at me, speechless (if you knew how much these girls could talk, then you'd understand that this was a serious matter). Their eyes directed mine towards the trampoline and to the problem at hand.

I looked up and immediately spotted the issue. I tried to keep my eyes fixed on Ahmed's face, who was concentrating on his basic moves on the trampoline. I desperately needed to catch his attention while trying to exude an air of normality (successfully I hoped). Everyone was too busy being transfixed by the girl's silence on the floor to notice anything untoward happening elsewhere. I waved him over, he stopped bouncing (thank God) and came towards me. With my head held high, and eyes still transfixed on his, he squatted down in front of me (wrong move). Don't let your eyes drop, was all I kept telling myself.

He leaned in towards me, and all I could whisper was, "You've fallen out of your underwear. Would you mind dressing yourself, please?"

"Ok," he said, and nodded as if I'd asked him to put the equipment away. Well in a way, I had. Without it sounding too crass, he appeared to be very well-developed for his age (part of the reason for the girl's reactions, I think). He hopped off the trampoline, went to the equipment cupboard, tucked himself back in, returned, and then climbed back on the trampoline as if nothing had happened. I had to resume the lesson as though this was par for the course. From that day, the pupils and students received an underwear dress code warning before every lesson.

This has continued throughout my career.

Dave just stood there with mouth opened. I ended my story with; "And I bet he doesn't remember that."

THE LAKE DISTRICT TRIP

It was the second week of a new academic year. Previously, in conjunction with the local Premier football league's NCS (National Citizenship Service) staff, the sports staff had successfully organised and completed a residential outdoor education activity. It was deemed so successful that it was to be repeated and scaled up the following year. The compulsory volunteers were to be made up of 150 students who had applied and accepted places on courses within the Care and Sport Curriculum area.

We were after all ticking lots of OFSTED (Office for Standards in Education, Children's Services and Skills) boxes on enrichment, employability, community work, inclusion, voluntary work... the list goes on.

I'm sure you can imagine that this was not to be an easy undertaking. Risk assessments needed to be written, contacts to be made with partner schools about the new students, covering the whole gamut of backgrounds including mental, physical, health, culture and religious information. The preparations seemed endless and therefore had to begin in the summer term of the then pupils last year at school. So there were also extensive parent/staff meetings. Some of the parents expressed their nervousness at relinquishing the responsibilities of their precious bundles into the hands of untested new staff. The fact that some of the children had never even ventured unescorted into the city centre or left the city boundaries meant the situation required very delicate negotiations. These conversations proceeded slowly with caution. In fact, one parent even asked me if he could go on the trip too. The offer was politely refused, knowing that he wouldn't have asked if it was his son and not his daughter attending the trip. The students were to spend four nights in the Lake District, then on their return complete a number of voluntary hours to gain their full NCS qualification.

This was unlike any of my previous trips; I was not one of the lead organisers, had little knowledge of the planning and no knowledge of the student's individual idiosyncrasies. I was used to male sport students and these were in the majority female health students (believe me, this made a huge difference). I had a wealth of knowledge of the typical types of behaviours displayed during activities and downtime with sports boys, therefore my experience was quite niche.

I had a particular system when it came to residentials; I needed all the information and needed to be fully involved in the planning. I didn't necessarily want to be running it, just fully informed.

As my expertise was not required in the initial planning, I therefore presumed that I was not participating in the residential. I was under the illusion that as some of the students were in my subject area that I was just helping out with the meetings where necessary. How wrong I was. just before college finished for the summer, I was told by senior management that as our most experienced member of staff regarding residentials, I would be attending.

Thanks.

As Rumsfeld has said I found myself "in the unknown knowns...". Having reviewed some of the background information, I was now particularly uneasy with the group of students that I had inherited: there were some serious medical and behavioural issues. Even more worrying was the fact that I was working with non-sports staff who had never worked on a residential, so had no idea what was in store. I'm sure some even thought that it might be a bit of a jolly.

With the variety of physical activities, challenges, behavioural issues and the sleep disturbance that they were about to encounter: what could possibly go wrong?

Many of the girls were BAME (Black and Minority Ethnic) Muslim students, and as previously stated, some had rarely travelled across the city; if they had, they were escorted, and indeed some were escorted to college by older relatives. Many displayed their disinterest in any sport. You can see that I'm painting a positive picture here. The mix of Sports (boys) and Health and Social Care (girls) was certainly going to be interesting.

Day One

The day had arrived. On our second head count we discovered that we had a stowaway. This student had the fortitude to put her bags into the hold, step onto the coach, sit down and be non-responsive during the register and head count. Why would she do that? Remember my previous statement of not being in charge and having little organisational knowledge of the trip? My suggestion was that parents would be called, she would be taken off the coach with her bags and there would be some form of investigation or disciplinary procedure in place on our return.

This didn't happen. She insisted that she had brought her paperwork in, implying therefore that the fault was in our hands. She managed to convince the organisers that she was genuine and was therefore allowed to go. (What are we setting ourselves up for? I thought). She couldn't participate in any of the activities, however, until all of her paperwork had arrived. This was to be brought up by a senior member of staff a day later as there was no fax machine in the residential buildings.

The knock-on effect here was that due to her nonparticipation status, she could not be left alone in the building. Therefore, a member of staff had to be allocated to stay with her, so affecting the staff/student ratio. This logistical nightmare added to my 'Told you so' smugness and 'Why didn't you listen to what I said?' suggestion, but I couldn't allow myself to dwell on this as we now had to rejig staffing and would be a staff member down for the practical activities.

Back to the coach journey: it was fairly uneventful until about an hour into the journey. I heard a commotion from the middle of the coach and went to investigate. A few of the girls pointed into the distance, "What's that?" I looked in the direction of their faces but all I could see were sheep grazing. I looked again as they continued to get more animated. I still couldn't see what they were pointing at and thought that it must be my older eyesight. I asked them to describe what they were seeing.

"Those things in the fields that look really woolly."

Time stood still, or so it seemed. The subject of their excitement had dawned on me. They had never seen sheep before. I looked at them and thought, surely everyone has seen sheep, even on TV. Even more poignant is the fact that Sheffield was surrounded by countryside and all manner of livestock. I realised that these girls were even more sheltered than I had thought. Today, their education had really begun. Who knew what the next few days would bring?

We were travelling in three coaches, two single-sex and one mixed, where there were no objections from parents. On the mixed coach, the girls needed to be dropped off at their accommodation first. One of the conditions for some of the girls being able to attend was that boys and girls would stay in separate accommodation. We had managed to secure two youth hostels, ten miles apart (much to the pleasure of the parents, of course). As we approached the hostel, I received a message that the students would not be able to alight directly in front of the accommodation as the road was too steep and narrow. The coach would therefore have to park at the bottom of the hill. We were to walk up the remainder of the way with our luggage. Text messages flew across the coaches and panic quickly ensued. Test number one: how to get the girls up to the accommodation without too much trauma. Well, I'd failed before I even started. As soon as they saw the hill, there were screams of "I can't get up that mountain with my bags!", "Who's going to carry this for me?" and "Where's my dad?"

All I kept thinking was, you don't get this with the sports boys. I had to employ my most engaging teacher speak and tone to distract them, while I thought, What on earth would the remaining days be like if they can't even walk up the hill? A few of the girls had to stop halfway for a rest. I was already losing patience and at one point resorted to the laying on of hands with the slowest student; one hand resting in the middle of her back and gently pushing her up the hill while simultaneously maintaining pressure to prevent her from slowing to a stop. At the same time, I was carrying two sets of bags and giving words of e-n-c-o-u-r-a-g-e-m-e-n-t (can you feel the frustration?). I didn't ask for this, I chuntered in my head. I'm only here because I'm the most experienced member of staff and senior management were now looking to me to lead the team, despite leaving me out of the planning. Please let this week be without too much drama, I inwardly begged.

The following morning, my allocated group were on their hiking day for their first activity. I assumed it would be the usual issues of kit sorting... or so I thought. Normally there are the usual queries regarding kit sizes: boots being too tight, helmets too small or waterproofs having holes in them... not this time.

"They're not this year's colour, I can't wear these."

"Why are the waterproofs so stiff?"

"Why do they smell so bad?"

"I've got to carry all of this?"

"I can't walk in these boots; they don't match my clothes."

Then came the line that stumped me.

As we were finally ready to depart, I noticed that one of the girl's boot laces were undone; she was actually shuffling along behind everyone else with her daypack and waterproofs hanging off her shoulders.

"Ayaan, stop. You need to do your laces," I shouted to her.

"I know."

She carried on shuffling. I caught up to her and stopped her.

"You can't go any further without doing them up. I'll wait with you and we can catch the others up." She stood there, looked at her boots, then slowly looked at me. She then uttered words that I would never have expected to hear from anyone of her age.

"Can you do them for me?"

I looked at her then turned around and looked at the space behind me, because surely she wasn't referring to me.

She was.

A long pause ensued.

"I'm sorry," I said. I really could not think of how else to reply without wanting to snap (different thoughts were running through my head: how dare she? Who does she think she is? What does she think I'm here for?)

"That's not my job," was all that I could muster.

"I don't know how to do them. My dad always ties them for me."

I was stumped.

She was sixteen.

She was serious, she really couldn't tie her laces. What the hell did her father think he was doing? It's a fundamental skill that every child should learn. I could go on, but we had a situation that needed resolving and the group was now disappearing into the distance. Well, I was the teacher and although I'd never envisaged teaching this skill to teenagers, it had to be done. So I taught her to tie her laces. Verbally.

It was as painful to instruct as it was to watch but, task completed we had to hurry and catch up with our group. Ayaan was picking up the rear with her daypack and waterproofs fashionably hanging off her shoulders, but at least her laces were tied.

The walk continued smoothly enough, until I heard a scream, followed by shouts. I raced ahead to see what the commotion was all about. As I approached the group, I scanned the area but couldn't see anything. Then I saw one of the girls screaming while looking at the ground. I still couldn't see anything.

"What's that? I don't like them." I looked again, nothing out of the ordinary. "Look at that!"

I looked. All I saw were ants. I looked at her. "Do you mean these?" I pointed at them.

"Yes," came the hysterical reply. Well, I thought, this residential has only just started but it was already the unwanted gift that keeps on giving. I had to compose myself before I could find an appropriate reply, but before I could, out came a demand.

"I want a taxi."

That was it, I lost my composure. My hands spanned outwards to show her the beautiful Lake District hills and I said: "Can you see any roads here? And as for the ants, you also have them in your house. They won't harm you." Well, they could bite, I thought, but I wasn't about to give that message out. This was just our first activity on day one. I again reminded myself of how much I knew and understood the peculiarities of the sports students, particularly the boys, and how this was certainly not the case for the Health girls; they were definitely the unknown quantity. Well, I was certainly beginning to find that out.

Day Two: Abseiling, what could happen today?

With full stomachs and having had our kit distributed, we made our way to the next challenge. The students were in a jovial mood, unaware of their next activity. We meandered through trees, clamoured over a few rocks and emerged at the activity site. I watched their faces as the girls realised the enormity of their next task. It's always a challenge when students take their first look over a bridge or viaduct and see the height that they have to descend. The banter stopped and became swiftly replaced with high-pitched panicked noises. I witnessed the changes in body language and overheard the heightened conversations that were quickly followed by a consensus of non-participation. The instructors were unable to coax any of the party over the edge.

I had to step up and abseil first (it's my usual ploy anyway), but I still had to coax the students into the harnesses and off the ledge. Ayaan is again the focal point of my story. She was one of the last students to complete her abseil. We were abseiling over a viaduct; the initial section is the most difficult with the latter section being a free swing of about thirty metres or so. So, I suppose if you're not used to it there is the utter panic of worrying if the ropes will hold your weight. As Ayaan stepped over the barrier she was visibly shaking, so she was given small, continuous instructions to help to maintain her focus. As she was preparing to let go all I could hear was her increasing vocal tones of "Oh my Go(de), oh my Go(de)," with her English gaining a more pronounced Somalian accent in symmetry with her increasing anxiety. As she descended, her legs swung freely as they were no longer in contact with the bridge section. Her exclamations of "Oh my God(e)" increased even more when she realised that her vocal support had disappeared. The (de) is important here as it became more exaggerated and sounded like the beginnings of the word death. This continued for some time; the safety rope had eventually slackened but the noise had not. I looked over the viaduct and shouted, "Ayaan, you can stop the noises now as you've reached the ground."

To her astonishment, she looked down and realised she was on terra firma. A huge beam spread across her face as she realised her accomplishment and she strutted across to her mates, exclaiming how easy it was. That kind of success always makes the evenings more enjoyable as the students regaled stories of their achievements throughout the day.

Back at the youth hostel, we were getting ready for our evening meal. The Senior Leadership Team were completing their nightly change over. Tonight, we were being graced with the presence of the principal and the vice principal. While in the dinner queue, I was reviewing the day with them, expressing my views on the events so far and the amazing opportunities given to the Muslim girls in particular, as they were able to let their hair down (literally), and enjoy a small modicum of freedom, when we heard a horrible scream. We ran around the corner in the general direction of the noise and I remember moving people out of the way to get to what I thought was a student in distress.

I stopped abruptly; in front of me could only be described as a site not unlike a St Trinians film. There was Ayaan (again), arms in the air, screaming that she needed medical attention as her face was on fire.

"My face is on fire, I need an ambulance," she demanded.

Her face was totally covered in a yellow lumpy substance. I kept my distance as there was still an element of anger and general commotion around her and I needed to think as to how I was going to tackle the situation. We then started to separate the students off into different sections of the building, those for interview and the others to their rooms to quell the situation. I was still confused by the product on her face and, with the amount of pain that she was expressing, I soon realised that it was more shock than pain. That's when I spotted it. Ayaan looked as though she had been viciously attacked by an outbreak of pale chicken pox but when my eyes scanned down to the table, I saw the offending article. The pudding bowl. A small chuckle exited from my mouth, then I remembered that I was the responsible adult and needed to keep control.

Her face was covered in apple crumble and custard.

The voice in my head questioned, Mmm to wipe it off or eat the remainder in the bowl? It couldn't have happened to a nicer girl to be honest. She got the attention that she desired but not the medical attention that she sought. During the investigation we discovered that she had been pestering a fellow student for most of the evening; this had escalated during the meal and the only weapon that this girl had to hand was her pudding. I would have thought twice about wasting my favourite pudding on someone's face. I might have used someone else's though.

Day Three

As much as I would have liked to change groups, just to see how everyone else was getting on, I remained with my group for the remainder of the activities. Today, we were kayaking and canoeing. My group of mainly Somalian Muslim girls were about to enter the water (definitely unknown territory). The previous night, the staff were discussing the issues around the girls and the need for female leads for the activities. We were short of these, so we had to think of compromises while still ensuring that their cultural and religious needs were met and respected.

That morning the girls weren't happy and were trying all the tricks in the book to avoid the activity: "I'm on my period, I feel really ill, I didn't sleep last night, I can't eat my breakfast, I have no energy, I'm scared of water, I'm too big, you haven't got a wetsuit my size." All of these we had an answer for. They eventually had to concede as the staff were not easily fooled. The girls were taking part in the activity whatever the excuses were.

They yielded and decided that the activity was fine, as long as they were fully covered from head to toe. This meant wetsuits and additional clothing to hide any exposed areas.

Finally, the girls were dressed, canoes packed and off we went in the minibus to the lake. The canoes were unloaded and placed near the jetty, groups were chosen and staff tried to match weight with confidence. For additional safety and buoyancy, two canoes were strapped together, which made it more difficult for them to tip into the water. Everyone was relatively happy with their groups, so we set off to launch the canoes into the lake.

At the front of the queue, four of the girls immediately went and sat in their canoes. I stood at the back, watching and waiting. I waited a little more but no one had said anything, so I then approached them.

"How are you going to get into the water?"

They looked at me as if I was speaking a foreign language.

"The water won't come to you. You have to go to it by launching the canoes off the jetty."

I watched as the lightbulbs gradually went on. They all got out of the canoes and slowly carried them down to the edge. One of the girls decided that she would direct the group, so stood in the middle of the two strapped canoes facing the girls with her back to the water, barking orders. I could see what was going to happen, but these girls were oblivious to the possible hazard. I had to think quickly if I was to halt the proceedings but decided that the water would be too shallow to cause any lasting damage.

They continued to slowly make their way towards the edge of the jetty and were descending the steepest section. Their self-proclaimed leader was still in between the two canoes giving directions. She suddenly realised that the water was around her ankles and her eyes widened as the rest of the group continued to struggle with the weight of the canoes, oblivious to the unfolding scene. She was now trapped between two canoes and the water's edge and suddenly realised that there could only be one ending.

She had no choice but to give in to the forward march of her peers and allow herself to be swallowed up by the water. Her arms flayed backwards as the straps hit her legs. She screamed as she started to lose her balance and toppled into the water, causing her team to look up, they then realised what was happening. They screamed too.

I let my body give in to the convulsions of laughter that were quickly immersing me. I walked over towards the commotion and soon realised that the screams had changed to laughter. The three girls carrying the canoes had dropped them and were bent double howling as they stared at their friend. I continued to approach, then understood the change in emotion. Their leader was flaying about in the water on her back, still screaming with a desperate look on her face, but going nowhere. She was in about three centimetres of water. She looked at me, realising that I was standing next to her, and was suddenly silent. I stood over her, bent down, put my hand on her shoulder and told her that she was going to be ok.

She stopped, looked at me, looked at her surroundings, then at the girls, and burst out laughing while continuing to fake her previous drowning movements.

This event broke the ice for the remainder of the day and they all happily participated in the water events. They stood on their canoes, chased and splashed each other and, unbelievably, jumped in and out of the lake for the remainder of the session.

Who would have guessed how this was to end? Some of the students certainly had moments to remember.

So, where were the boys in all of this? About ten miles away through winding dark roads in another youth hostel. I made the return journey every night to support both staff and students.

One of the nights I overheard some of the boys planning to visit the girls. I smiled and just dropped a hint at the twenty-mile return journey over a few hills in the dark. Oh, and no lights anywhere.

The look of dismay on their faces.

AARON'S DENIAL

."Oi, ...Oi...OI mate."

Aaron thinks to himself I don't know anyone who speaks like that so they can't be talking to me.

There's a tap on his shoulder.

"Are you Maxine's son?"

He immediately replies, "Don't know what you're talking about mate."

(He studied at my place of work)

GLOSSARY OF USEFUL TERMS

Chuntering: talk or grumble, maybe in increasing tones. Just ask my hubby Dave, he's the expert.

Land based College: specializing in agriculture, horticulture, equine studies, fisheries, gamekeeping, sport (I don't know why they decided that this was a good fit here).

Level 2 students: generally, students who have not passed all of their qualifications during compulsory school education to get to Level 3, or they're just taking a little longer for a multitude of reasons.

Level 3 students: pre university qualifications.

Porter cabin: temporary office/classroom space, depending on the state of education it can be a semi-permanent classroom.

Viva: a professional discussion to assess competencies.

AFTERWARDS

So, you think this residential malarky is a bit of a jolly do you? Well, Gail and I find ourselves yet again, sitting out in the middle of a corridor in the middle of the night. We're not looking our best; we've positioned ourselves between the boys and girls section and are wearing our carefully selected jimjams; we checked to make sure that it covers all manner of sins. We're waiting for our unsuspecting students who are trying to flit between the girls and the boys dorm.

ACKNOWLEDGEMENTS

To my family and friends who listened to these stories time and time again.

To, Rachael Batty, Anthony Bonney, Holly Bradley, Ben Bradshaw, Mel Bridger, Janine Dyer, Jayde Jarrett-Pearson, Aileen Jarret-Ward, Amanda Lenon, Janine Roberts and Jeanette Ruiz, for your critical eyes and advice.